MAKE IT
ALL ABOUT
THEM

MAKE IT ALL ABOUT THEM

{ **WINNING SALES PRESENTATIONS** }

NADINE KELLER

WILEY

John Wiley & Sons, Inc.

To the men in my life:

*My dad, my husband Peter, and my two phenomenal boys,
PK and Christopher*

Contents

Acknowledgments

Thank you everyone at Wiley, especially you, Daniel Ambrosio for finding me! Christine Moore, my goal is to channel you!

I am so grateful for my husband Peter, and my two boys, PK and Christopher. I will never forget our first editorial session, on a beautiful summer day in the field, as we scoured the first 30,000 words! Thank you for your love and support throughout this process and for always being champions of my career. I am so proud! Christopher—who knew that a teenage boy could be a responsible and insightful intern to his own mother? You did a great job (except for that day when you fell asleep reading my manuscript). I think we broke records, and your editing skills make it easier to write those tuition checks!

Melinda—you make me laugh every day. It seems such a cliché to say that you are the wind beneath my wings, but, what the heck, *you are*—and you always have been.

Dad—you are my number-one cheerleader . . . even at age 94!

Linda Knox, Kathleen Johnson, Kristin Arnold, and Erin Hubbard you inspire me. Thanks, girlfriends!

Eric Baron—you are the master! Thank you for your generosity and support over the years.

Denise, HT, Ian, Ron, Lionel, and Jim, thank you for your contributions.

Thanks, Trish Loger, for your wonderful cartoons, and Doug Barron, for all your help on this and all other projects, old and new.

I am honored to be a coach to many wonderful professionals. Thank you for allowing me into your lives. It has been my privilege, and I have learned so much!

Introduction: Creating an Experience

We have been boring each other for years during sales presentations.

If you have ever been a member of a buying committee, you surely know what it's like to sit through a page-by-page turn of a presentation that is more easily measured in pounds than ounces.

Perhaps you have heard salespeople drone on about the size of their firm, their clients, and their products. Or watched some poor souls read bullet point after bullet point of detailed information about their company that is of little interest to their audience.

Maybe you've witnessed someone respond to a simple yes-or-no question with a five-minute response that never really seems to answer the initial query. Or you may have even experienced that awkward and uncomfortable moment when a member of the buying committee says to the sales team, "I am sorry, but we are going to have to end now. Your time is up." Yikes!

These scenarios are abundant in sales presentations. They often come as a result of unstated traditions, myths, and rules that have been so ingrained in corporate America that they have become commonplace.

Let's face it, the bar has been set low—very low.

And because these scenarios are often accepted behavior, people have been successful in spite of it.

Early in my career, I was responsible for the investor, client, and employee communications for a man named Bill Harrison, who was the vice chairman of the Chase Manhattan's Global Bank. It was just after the Chemical–Chase merger, and several years before the JPMorgan–Chase merger. Bill later became the Chairman of JPMorgan Chase. I would love to tell you I had something to do with the man's success, but I would be lying. In fact, looking back at it, I consider myself an accessory to the popular crime of the day— "murder by PowerPoint." I loaded him up with slide after slide and bullet point after bullet point until his warm and charming personality was so diluted that there was little or no chance of his connecting with his audience. Sorry, Bill.

It was hardly a career-breaking approach. In fact, his presentations looked like every other soon-to-be-chairman type back in the 1990s. To be honest, not much has changed since then (with a few notable exceptions, such as Steve Jobs.) So, the question becomes, "If you can still be successful in the traditional presentation approach, then why bother to change?" My answer is, "Because doing so brings huge opportunities."

It is harder than ever, in today's commodity-based world, to differentiate ourselves from the competition. The experience that we create for our prospects in a sales presentation can be that sought-after point of differentiation—and can be the difference between winning and losing deals.

Creating this experience has a lot less to do with what we say than with how we say it. Yet when salespeople and teams prepare for sales presentations, they focus most of their time and energy on the content (i.e., the *what*) and very little on the experience (i.e., the *how*).

There has been a substantial shift to focusing on customer experience over the past 10 years or so. In fact, most of our clients have appointed so-called experience officers. A client of mine named Linda Knox is responsible for the intermediary experience at Prudential Retirement. In a paper that she wrote to help define *experience* for the organization, she noted that "with the commoditization of products and services, differentiation has become elusive—the Holy Grail all companies seek." She further states that the "ability to stage experience is the gateway to differentiation." Linda takes this concept to an extraordinary level by very consciously designing the desired experience for every interaction a client or intermediary has with Prudential Retirement. Several years ago, she led a team that created a homelike environment in their Hartford office building to use for client meetings and site visits. They actually renovated about 1,200 square feet of space in their office building to mimic a warm yet contemporary space that resembles someone's home—complete with a front door, a living room, a kitchen and a dining room—conference area. Every detail, from the scents that are created by diffusers to the sound of the doorbell at the front door to what is written on the blackboard in the kitchen to the ice cream loaded in the freezer, was designed with experience in mind.

In their book *The Experience Economy: Work Is Theater & Every Business a Stage* (B. Joseph Pine II and James H. Gilmore, Harvard Business Press, 1999), Pine and Gilmore argue that businesses must orchestrate memorable events for their customers and that memory itself becomes the product—the experience. They suggest that there is concrete economic value in experience, as it allows a company to truly differentiate from its competition.

Pine and Gilmore write, "While commodities are fungible, goods tangible and services intangible, experiences are memorable." They suggest that most parents don't take their kids to Walt Disney World just for the event itself, but rather to make that shared experience part of everyday family conversations for months, even years, afterward. They explain, "While the experience itself lacks tangibility, people greatly value the offering because its value lies within them, where it remains long afterward."

A great example of how an experience can be game changing is former vice president Al Gore's film project, *An Inconvenient Truth*. During the 2000 presidential campaign—and for many years leading up to it—Gore touted the dangers of global warming without much fanfare. On losing the election, he devoted his full energies to creating awareness around the topic. He hired a California-based firm, Duarte, to help him create a story and develop a slide show. The presentation was so powerful that it was later made into a film that received an Academy Award and a Nobel Peace Prize.

The moral of the story is that Gore did not change what he said; he changed how he said it. He created an experience for the audience unlike any other. And he became a rock star as a result.

So, how does this translate to the sales presentation? We sometimes forget why prospects often spend thousands of dollars and invest many hours in final presentations. They want to experience the team—and what it would be like to work with you. Now, they may not use these exact words; they may not even be conscious of it. But that is what it essentially boils down to. If it were solely about the facts and the figures, we could save everyone a lot of time and money by just sending them the presentation in an e-mail and calling it a day. Better yet, they would make the decision based on the request for proposal (RFP) response.

It is crucial to remember that buying decisions are largely based on emotion. Back in the 1950s, many companies and brands assumed that consumers made purchasing decisions based on the facts. So Madison Avenue (which now conjures up images from the popular cable show *Mad Men*) was busy creating advertising designed to convince consumers that one product worked better than another product.

Today, it is widely understood and documented that emotions play a significant role in buying decisions. In the late 1990s, science and technology gave way to a new field of marketing, developed by Harvard psychologists, called *neuromarketing*—the science of analyzing brain activity in decision making. Researchers use technologies such as MRIs and EEGs to measure brain patterns that demonstrate the link between emotions and decision making. Companies such as Google and Frito Lay are currently using this technology to test their messages in the marketplace.

Of course, I'm not suggesting that you hook up the entire buying committee to an EEG. However, I am suggesting that we need to spend a lot more time thinking through how we impact the emotions of our buyers in a sales presentation.

The Sales Presentation Experience

Three components contribute to the sales presentation experience: the messages we communicate, the behaviors (and skills) we exhibit, and the materials we use. The messages are the *what*; the behaviors, skills, and materials are the *how*. All three components should help us make emotional connections with the audience.

This book is divided into three sections based on these components. It is meant to break down years of myths and traditions under which salespeople have labored and to point out rules that are meant to be broken. By applying the tips, tools, and techniques outlined within each chapter, salespeople can break through the "we have always done it this way" mentality that is so prevalent in corporate America and provide a truly unique and differentiated sales presentation experience that will ultimately result in winning presentations.

Section 1 focuses on how to identify the key messages for your clients. Section 2 explores how to deliver those messages in the most memorable, engaging, and compelling way. Section 3 addresses how to use materials so they drive home your messages and support your personal and emotional connection with the client. Also included is a section that outlines all the components that will impact the presentation experience and a simple tool kit designed to help you immediately apply this winning approach.

MAKE IT ALL ABOUT THEM

What You Present: The Messages

Make It All About Them

Myth: It's all about us.
Truth: It's all about them.

The most common misconception about the sales presentation is that the prospects want to hear all about us, the company presenting: our size, our clients, our products, our people, and our awards. In fact, this is so ingrained in corporate sales culture that clients actually feed into these misconceptions—so much so that they provide direction or issue agendas that make everyone think that they want the presentation to be all about the firm that is selling the products and services. They ask us to explain our products and services, they ask us to tell them how we are different, and they ask us to tell them about our processes and systems. Yet, in reality, clients want the presentation to be about *them*. They want to hear how we are going to help them to solve their problems, address their needs, and seize their opportunities. They want to be the center of the story. Think about it: Most of us have been on the buying side at one time or another. A sales presentation that is all about the vendor and the product is a big bore. A sales presentation that focuses on the audience and their problems, on the other hand, is engaging.

Recently, my husband and I interviewed financial advisors. We were rolling over a 401(k) from a previous employer and thought it would make sense to consolidate our investments. We interviewed two advisors, and the contrast between the two was notable. We spent considerable time reviewing our situation with each, and the first began his discussion with an overview of his background and his firm's capabilities. He then said that he had looked at our portfolio and would recommend several mutual funds based on his review. He went on to talk about the funds—their track record, management fees, and so forth. In contrast, the other advisor started by confirming what he knew about our particular situation and then continued with a series of questions. He asked us to talk about our biggest short-term concerns and our vision for the future. At the end of this, he summarized our situation as if he had known us for years. He went on with several recommendations, tying them into our needs, fears, dreams, and realities. When he left, my husband and I knew he was the guy for us. It didn't really have much to do with his recommendations (although they were certainly on target). Rather, it was his ability to demonstrate that he understood what was important to us—after just one encounter—that impressed us so greatly.

My colleague Kent Reilly brings the concept of making it all about the client to life with the following analogy that I have borrowed many times. Imagine that you ran into a friend after a party that you had both attended. He whips out his iPad to show you pictures from the party. As you scroll through, Kent asks, which pictures do you think will most hold your interest? If you are like most people, you will answer—pictures of you!

Maybe you can better relate to a situation in which a host at a dinner party offers to share the family vacation slides (yes, one of those), and you have that sudden and urgent need to get that extra glass of wine to help you through the next 20 minutes. Do you think you would feel differently about those slides if you had been along on that vacation? Of course you would. Stories, like slide shows and photo albums, are much more interesting to you if you are in them.

This is why we need to make our clients the stars of the photo album—and then show them how we fit into their pictures, not the other way around. In short, *we need to make it all about them.*

"Ok, enough about us, what *do you* think about us?"

Old tradition: Begin the content of the presentation with your stats.

New tradition: Begin the content of the presentation with their needs.

Because so many people think that clients want to hear all about us, the tendency is to kick off the presentation talking all about us. I have seen far too many introductory slides with bullet points detailing the company's history, scale, and clients. Is this the most important and engaging information that we can give the client during those critical first few moments of a final presentation? Of course not!

I have heard Eric Baron, president and founder of The Baron Group, a sales training firm in Westport, Connecticut, suggest many times that clients' first inclination to buy happens when they believe that the salesperson understands their needs.

I think we can all relate to an experience where we have been the prospect—whether we are buying a house, a new TV, or the services of a financial advisor. You know, that moment where the salesperson just seems to get what is important to you?

For example, I was recently in the market for a dishwasher to replace the dish drawers that we had installed in our kitchen about eight years ago. I thought this was going to be a pretty easy purchase—and I was completely wrong. After visiting several appliance stores and a couple of the big-box stores, I found out there are a lot of bad dishwashers out there. While checking reviews on the Internet, I happened across an online appliance store and decided to call. The salesperson began by asking me why I was in the market for a new dishwasher. I told him that my current dishwasher needed too many repairs and I was tired of all the service calls. He then asked me several more questions. After about 10 minutes, he said something like, "So, with two teenage boys in the house and a husband who loves to cook, you probably can easily run that dishwasher a couple of times a day. You also do a lot of entertaining, and the last thing you need is for the dishwasher to give out right before a holiday, like it did for you on Thanksgiving. Given how you describe your kitchen, I imagine that the style is important to you as well, am I right?" Bingo! This salesperson had obviously been listening—and had clearly understood my needs. I was now inclined to buy.

He went on to strongly suggest that I rethink my target price upward to buy what he considers the best dishwasher on the market—which cost about twice as much as the dishwasher I thought I would buy. I gave him my credit card information, and my new dishwasher arrived the next day. I couldn't be happier with it—and with my entire buying experience (in case you are wondering, it is a Miele).

This story illustrates how important it is to frame everything in the context of the prospect's needs. The first order of business in the sales presentation is to confirm those needs, because this frames the rest of the presentation.

I am going to assume if you are reading this book that you are well versed in the importance of eliciting as much information and insight as you can about your clients' needs before you present any solutions to them. In a complex sale—where the sales cycle is typically long—this process is likely to occur over time through research, analysis, and a series of contacts with the client. Your understanding and insight into the client's situation, problems, and needs provides a critical foundation to an effective sales presentation. Failing to do this puts you at a significant disadvantage.

Companies often retain my firm, Precision Sales Coaching and Training, to help coach a team through a sales presentation. When structuring the presentation, we always ensure that the team begins their discussion with their analysis of the client's needs, problems, and opportunities—demonstrating that they understand the client company and that this discussion will be all about addressing its needs. In other words—it will be the *client's* photo album, not ours. We encourage salespeople to put the client's needs into their own words so it does not look like a cut-and-paste job from the RFP, but rather a thoughtful reflection of their understanding and insight into their needs—something that adds value right off the bat.

Note that this is only an expression of clients' needs; it does not and should not include your solution to their needs. It is the frame for the discussion—a photo of the clients without you in it. I sometimes think of it as a contract between you and the clients stating why you are there and what you will be discussing.

Later in the book, you will find out how negatively I feel about text-heavy slides. However, I make an exception with these kinds of needs-related slides, because the words and their meaning are so critical. It is important, however, that you preface this portion of your presentation carefully and deliberately by saying something like this: "Before we begin, I would like to review our understanding of your situation and needs. Everything that we talk about today is about addressing these, so it is critically important that we get this right. I am going to ask you to pay close attention as I review the next slide, which is a series of bullet points. Afterward, I will ask you to tell me what, if anything, we missed or what we may have misinterpreted."

This type of preamble does a few things:

- It demands audience attention. You have said that it is "critically important," which are words that get most people to focus.
- You have specifically asked the audience to read along with you—for just a few brief moments. This instruction engages them in the content and sends the message that you will not be reading to them the entire meeting.
- It encourages the audience to really tune in to what you are about to say, because you have given them a heads-up that they will have a speaking role in a few minutes.
- It sends a very strong message that this presentation is about them, not a 60- or 90-minute infomercial all about you. They are going to be the stars of this show.

We occasionally get some resistance when we suggest this approach to sales teams, which can come in the form of the question, "What if we're wrong?" This is particularly concerning in sales situations where an intermediary is involved, thereby limiting direct access to the clients.

My response is simple: "The clients will correct you." And it's important that you allow them to do so by asking them for feedback after you have reviewed your understanding of their needs. Be sure to encourage their response with a statement that invites discussion, similar to the following examples: "I'd like to pause here and ask you for some feedback." Or, "I'd like to hear your reaction to this." Statements like this will encourage clients to share information with you, as opposed to something more close-ended, such as, "Is this accurate?" (to which they can reply with a simple yes).

Often, you will gain new insights as they share their reactions—something that is particularly helpful if you are presenting after your competition has presented. The members of the buying committee are likely to have been influenced by things that they have liked or haven't liked during previous presentations. It is common for you to get a glimpse into their current thinking if you prompt them effectively—which can be gold to a sales team, because they can then adjust their comments directly to the client's newly acquired hot buttons.

This happened to me recently. We were the last of three vendors presenting to the buying committee of a small international bank that wanted to provide its bankers with sales training and coaching. We had done what we thought was a very thorough needs analysis. After reviewing our understanding of the client's needs, we paused and asked for feedback. The most senior member of the group shared the following: "We think our people struggle with time management." We asked him to elaborate. He told us that one of our competitors had talked about time management often being an issue with salespeople.

Well, time management was the last thing that we would have brought into this presentation had he not mentioned it. But this newfound knowledge allowed us to discuss how we address time management issues in our training programs. Had we not asked the question, we would never have known that the buying committee had identified and rearranged their priorities during the sales presentation process. They might have even decided to go with another vendor in this situation, assuming (incorrectly, of course) that we could not address their newly identified need for improved time management.

When buying committee members accept your invitation to add to or elaborate on the list of needs you've provided, it is critically important for you to accomplish the following:

- *Make sure you understand exactly what they are saying and why it is important to them.* When appropriate, ask them to elaborate or give a bit more detail on what they said. Ask follow-up questions so that you know how to address the need as you move forward in the presentation. This also demonstrates to the clients that you genuinely care about—and are paying close attention to—everything they have to say.
- *Capture the need so that you can refer to it later in the presentation.* In advance of the sales presentation, you may want to appoint one of your team members the role of ensuring that you address any new needs that surface somewhere in the body of the presentation.

- *Acknowledge it, but do not address it.* The objective of this exercise is to agree on what the clients' needs are and therefore what you will discuss in the meeting. All you need to do at this point is to thank them for their input, demonstrate that you heard them, and assure them that you will address it. For example, if a client were to say, "We also need to be certain that our current system will be compatible with your systems," the salesperson might reply, "Yes, compatibility is important to a smooth transition, and we will be certain to talk about how we interface with systems like yours when we get to technology. Thank you, Erin. Anything else?" Ideally, the salesperson or the person covering technology will circle back at the right time in the presentation and say something like, "Erin, you had mentioned in the opening that you were particularly interested in systems integration. . . ." After the session, he or she might then check in with anyone else who had questions that needed to be addressed.

If You Remember Only Three Things:

1. Begin every presentation by expressing your understanding of the clients' problems, needs, and opportunities.
2. Review each with them, explaining that since these are the basis for your presentation, you want to make sure that you have them right.
3. Elicit and take note of their feedback, and refer to it, as appropriate, during the presentation.

CHALLENGE

Begin your next presentation with your understanding of the client's problems, needs, and opportunities. Listen intently to the responses, and customize your comments throughout the presentation to what you have learned.

2 Start with the End in Mind

Tradition: When preparing for a presentation, open up the last presentation and begin to retrofit. (Hello, search and replace!)

Breaking tradition: Start with the end in mind.

I fully support being as efficient as possible when it comes to presenting. I do not expect any salesperson or team to start preparing for each sales presentation with a blank screen. Having said this, I know it serves salespeople and teams well when they invest even just 15 or 20 minutes to strategize before customizing a PowerPoint presentation for the new situation.

You should approach the sales-presentation experience as a story—one with a clear beginning, a middle, and an end. You must design every sales presentation based on the client to whom you are presenting—and what that client is trying to accomplish.

The single biggest mistake we see sales teams make when preparing for sales presentations is cramming too many messages into too little time. While they intellectually understand that it doesn't make sense, it is a hard habit to break for a number of reasons:

- We are proud of all of our stuff—and we want them to see it all!

"Since we only have an hour, I will talk fast."

- We are concerned that the competition will show them something that we don't—and (God forbid) they will think we don't have it.
- We just don't feel complete unless we show them everything.

The major problem with presenting too much information with too much detail in too little time is that we dilute our messages. The client is left confused and unable to understand how our offering is different from or better than the competition's—and, most important, why they should care.

The Power of Three

So, what is a sales team to do? First, start with the rule of three. We know that it is unrealistic to expect an audience to remember more than three things. This concept goes back as far as Aristotle, who wrote about it in his book *Rhetoric*, and its applications are everywhere we look. Think about it—there is magic to the number three.

In Fairy Tales:

- Three blind mice
- Three little pigs
- Goldilocks and the three bears

In Great Moments in History:

- Life, liberty, and the pursuit of happiness
- Blood, sweat, and tears
- I came; I saw; I conquered

In Public Safety:

- Stop, look, and listen.
- Stop, drop, and roll.
- Check, call, and care.

Even When There Is Just One Important Thing to Say, We Repeat It Three Times:

- It's all about location, location, location.
- "Our top priority . . . education, education, education [Tony Blair]."
- How do you get to Carnegie Hall? Practice, practice, practice.

And often, even when four things are stated, people will remember only three. The most famous example of this is Winton Churchill's "Blood, Sweat, and Tears" speech, in which he said, "I have nothing to offer but blood, toil, tears and sweat." So much for the toil!

Our brain is somehow programmed to easily remember groups of three. Push it to four, and it is on overload. I imagine that whatever is physiologically responsible for this in the human brain is made stronger by all the combinations of three that are introduced to us in childhood (e.g., A, B, C; 1, 2, 3; do, re, mi).

Advertisers, comedians, and screenplay writers apply this rule. Sales teams who apply this rule will have a competitive advantage.

How do you determine what those three messages should be? Ask yourself, "If I could communicate only three things to this client, what would they be?"

You can answer that question by applying the following screening criteria.

What Are the Client Needs?

Any consultative salesperson knows that if you don't do your homework up front, you have a weak foundation for the close. The most critical part of this homework is the ability to understand and analyze clients' needs. Your understanding goes far beyond the request for proposal (RFP), which is limited to the stated needs. The most pressing needs (and where deals are closed) typically take place behind the scenes, and they are typically unstated. These may include things such as:

- To have a trusting partner (because they do not trust their current provider)
- To like their relationship manager (because they either love or hate their current one)
- To be perceived as making a good decision (because the last one didn't work out so well)
- To find a provider who has bandwidth (because they are likely to be acquiring)
- To have a partner who is committed to the business (because they suspect their current provider is not investing)

An analysis of both stated and unstated needs therefore becomes the first filter you can use to determine your three messages.

What Are Our Strengths?

With client needs as background, the next things to assess are our strengths against the clients' needs. Specifically, we must ask ourselves, "Where can we really shine?" Think about client feedback and the reasons that you have won past deals. Think about client research that is available and awards and recognitions that you have won. Most important, think about this particular client's needs, problems, and opportunities and how you are positioned to help.

What Are Competitors' Strengths and Weaknesses?

Finally, we want to consider the competitors' strengths. What are competitors most likely to highlight in their presentations? And, most important, what are their weaknesses in relation to the client's stated and unstated needs and our strengths? Where are their vulnerabilities?

This analysis will allow you to identify your three big messages, which then serve as the compass for your presentation. You can now weave them into each section of the presentation so that later, when the buying committee is reviewing what you had to say, they have clarity on who you are and why they should hire you. The following exercise is designed to help you select your three messages.

The "How to Choose Just Three" Exercise

With your team, discuss:

1. The client's needs
2. Your strengths
3. The competitors' strengths and weaknesses

With these three screens as background, brainstorm with the team potential ideas for the key messages. Don't worry about choosing the final three at this point—you will do that later.

Encourage the use of real language rather than corporate jargon. Here are some examples:

- We get you!
- You'll be a big fish in a small pond!
- We want to work with you!

- We can grow with you!
- We can make your life easier.
- We are the safe choice.
- We are easy to work with.
- We have the track record.
- We are like you (culturally aligned).
- We know how to do this!
- We have the international experience that you need.
- Our approach will save you money in the long run.
- We are worth our higher fees.
- We've got your back.

Once your ideas are exhausted, review the list to see which messages begin to emerge as most compelling. Test them against the screening criteria. It usually becomes clear at this point, and you can refine the messages if necessary. Do not wordsmith or edit too intensely for the client at this point; just make sure the team understands the essence of the messages.

Assure the team that the messages that you do not choose will nonetheless be an important part of the presentation. The idea here is to answer the question, "If we had only three messages to deliver to the client, what would they be?" And yes, answering this question, and deciding to emphasize just three messages takes guts. You and/or the team are likely to feel concerned that you are limiting your presentation, as there may be concern that the competition may cover something that you are leaving out. But have confidence in your approach. Keep in mind as well that some team members will want to choose more than three. Expect that people will want to combine two or more messages into one (this is cheating!). Be ruthless, and stick to your rule here. It will pay off in the end. Remember, the idea is to provide clarity to clients about who you are and why they should choose you. More than three messages will dilute your entire presentation.

One of the greatest benefits to this technique is that in addition to helping to project clarity of your messaging throughout the entire presentation, it also provides a powerful close. And teams often struggle with how to close their presentation.

It is not uncommon for a team to find that they are left with as little as a minute or two to close. While we always suggest that teams manage their time closely, we also know that running out of time is a common occurrence, even for the best of us. Having the three key messages in your back pocket can provide a quick close if need be, since you can easily shorten or expand them to fit the time remaining. Let's look at an example.

> On behalf of the team, I want to thank you again for your time today. We know that this is an important decision for you, and we have covered a lot of ground. We are, of course, available to continue our discussion and answer any questions that you may have. With that said, if we could leave you only three things from our presentation today, they are:
> 1. One, we understand you! We have considerable experience in your industry and a track record of success addressing the challenges that you are facing. We can hit the ground running.
> 2. Two, we are in the business of making our clients lives easier—and we will do that for you. We know that there has been a strain on your system, and we can take care of that—quickly.
> 3. And finally, we have your back. We are known throughout the industry for our rigorous standards and attention to detail, so you can sleep at night knowing that we are watching every detail.

Ideally, these messages will have been incorporated during the presentation, and this closing is a summary of what they have already been hearing, feeling, and thinking throughout.

Now that you have the three key messages, let's also touch on the importance of emotions in the buying process. Use the following simple, five-minute exercise to key into the emotional responses you want to trigger. I call it the "Reviews Exercise."

The Reviews Exercise

After a presentation, when the sales team leaves the room, a conversation usually takes place among the buying committee. This conversation might happen in a taxi, a train, or a plane if the buying committee has traveled to the sales team's office. But wherever it occurs, this conversation is typically not about the content they heard during the presentation. It tends to be more about how the committee feels about the team (or the experience), and it usually includes these kinds of comments:

- "Wow, I really liked them."
- "They seem like they would be great to work with."
- "They really get us."
- "What a nice group!"
- "They seem to really care."
- "They know their stuff."
- "They seemed to genuinely like each other."

With teams that I am coaching, I like to brainstorm what we'd want those comments to be. We then leave them up on a flip chart during the rehearsal so that we can remember that these are the emotions that we want to inspire.

With the three key messages identified and the reviews exercise completed, the salesperson and team are now ready to develop the story. Chapter 3 outlines a specific process for creating a storyboard that lays the foundation for a winning sales presentation.

If You Remember Only Three Things:

1. Before opening up the PowerPoint, determine the three most important messages for the client.

2. Analyze and capture how you want to impact the audience's emotions.
3. Use "the three messages" as a guide to determine what to include—and, most important, what to exclude—from your presentation.

CHALLENGE

Use "How to Choose Just Three" and the "Reviews Exercise" to prepare for your next sales presentation.

---

3 Develop a Story

Tradition: Prepare to deliver a sales presentation.
New tradition: Prepare to tell a story.

Storytelling is at the heart of impactful sales and marketing. There are three levels of stories to think about with a sales presentation.

THE STORIES WITHIN THE STORY
(Make It Real)

THE CLIENT'S STORY
(Make It About Them)

THE MARKETPLACE STORY
(Make It Clear)

The Three Levels of Story

There is the story that you tell the marketplace about who your company is and what you stand for. There are the stories you craft

21

for the specific clients to whom you are presenting. And there are the stories within the story, which bring what you do to life and makes it memorable for the client.

While the second and third levels of stories are most relevant to the sales presentation, it is important to not forget about the first. This serves as a foundational level that tells the marketplace what your company is about and who you are.

Many companies spend millions of dollars defining their brand and identity in the marketplace. Some are more successful than others. If you imagine Volvo, you immediately think of *safety*. Mention BMW, and you think of *performance*. Apple is about *innovation*, and W Hotels are *cool*. While your corporate brand is part of the story you tell the marketplace, it is not the only story. Your value proposition is just as important.

I define a *value proposition* very simply: It answers the client's question, "Why should we do business with you?" You always want to include the following in the value proposition:

- What you stand for
- How you are different
- What results your clients can expect

I call the value proposition a "stake-in-the-ground story," as it often requires people to make a difficult choice among several options. Since choosing just one can be stressful, many organizations are inclined to combine multiple ideas. However, this usually results in confusion in the marketplace. Calling it a stake-in-the-ground story reminds people how crucial it is to choose one concept, to build a story around it, and to be consistent and true to it.

I have found that, more often than not, businesses struggle with this. As a result, they often change their messages frequently or send out multiple messages, because they're unable to settle on one. But all this does is confuse current and potential customers about what your company does and the value it provides. It is particularly important to have a clear, simple-to-tell marketplace story, especially in sales models involving intermediaries. Since these situations depend largely on a third party to tell the story, clarity and consistency become paramount.

It is always preferable to have an imperfect story than no story at all, as the absence of a marketplace story comes with a price. In addition to creating confusion, lack of a story allows competitors, clients, and intermediaries to define your story for you—and it likely isn't the one you want to be telling.

Stake-in-the-ground stories are built around the strength of your offering and the value that you bring to your clients. You can build such a story from any of the following values:

- Performance and service
- Cost reduction
- Risk reduction
- Newness
- Accessibility
- Convenience
- Trust
- Design

Additionally, a strong stake-in-the-ground story will meet the following five criteria:

1. *It is compelling.* It is something that your target markets care enough about that they will be compelled to do business with you instead of with your competition.
2. *It is different from your competitor's story.* A great way to determine this is to ask yourself and your colleagues to think about the adjectives that the marketplace (competitors and clients) would use to describe your competitors. Steer clear of telling someone else's story.
3. *It is believable.* For instance, you clearly do not want to build your story around service if you have struggled with service issues and the marketplace knows it.

4. *It is achievable.* It is all right to stretch when you are telling your story, but you need to be able to deliver on it. Your organization's behavior will always trump any story, no matter how finely crafted.
5. *It is simple to understand and tell.* A third party—whether an intermediary or a client telling a colleague—should be able to easily repeat it.

After identifying the value upon which to build your story, I suggest that you write a paragraph or two from the perspective of your clients. In essence, ask yourselves, "What would clients say about us if we delivered on this story? How would they describe their experience working with us?" This helps to capture the concepts and behaviors that we want to highlight when we tell the story.

Once you have your stake in the ground, you must clearly and consistently reinforce it in every interaction that you have with the marketplace—including the sales presentation.

Your stake-in-the-ground story acts as the backdrop for your presentation and is one you tell consistently from client to client. It is important that the signals that you send and the behavior that you exhibit is consistent with the story. For example, we recently helped a small advisory firm establish such a story; at its core was the concept that this firm makes the complex simple. While its message has significant implications for all of its marketing materials, we focused most specifically on the finals presentation. We conducted a thorough review of the language, deleting all jargon and complicated wording. We also analyzed existing charts and redesigned them for simplicity and clarity. We even changed the font and colors and added simple imagery to drive home key concepts. We looked for opportunities to use analogies, metaphors, and stories that would clearly and simply outline the firm's capabilities. We did all of this because we knew that no matter how compelling the story, it would only truly be believed if we reinforced it with our behavior.

We did a similar project with a real estate and relocation firm whose stake-in-the-ground story was built around caring—specifically, the idea that this was the company that would take the best care of employees who were relocating. Once we identified the story, we wrote a brief paragraph (as I described earlier) as a client who was actually experiencing the relocation company's caring service:

> They really care about our people! They are committed to making our employees' moving experience as personal and stress-free as possible. This means that our transferees are partnered with people who really understand just how stressful a move can be, and they will have someone to hold their hand every step of the way. They and their families feel special and taken care of, and they appreciate that we (their employer) are providing this level of support.

This brief paragraph, gave us a lot to work with when building a presentation. Under the larger umbrella of caring, we could incorporate the concepts of commitment, personal service, stress-free relocation, partnership, understanding, feeling special, and appreciation.

We built the presentation from a blank screen, looking for every opportunity to embed caring concepts, languages, and images. The presentation began with the headline, "We move people with care," and we used images of people caring for others. We incorporated an audio of people who had been relocated talking about how they felt cared for during this stressful time in their lives. We highlighted the personal commitment of the day-to-day point person through anecdotes and stories. We made certain that every section of the presentation reinforced the caring concept, from the way the call center was managed to the way technology was designed.

Clarity around your value proposition is the first step in building a template for a presentation that consistently communicates to the marketplace who you are as a company and what you stand for. The next level of the story builds on that foundation and customizes it so that it resonates with the specific client to whom we are presenting.

The Presentation as a Story

Now that there is a foundational story to the marketplace on which the generic presentation is built, we need to think about how to customize it to a specific client. Every presentation to a client should be thought of as a story, with a beginning, a middle, and an end. We then need to use the power of storytelling to make it real, memorable, and interesting for the audience. Stories are an important part of creating the experience. We explore the art of storytelling in more detail—and discuss how to most effectively tell a story—in Chapter 7. For now, let's review how to structure a presentation as a story.

Creating a Storyboard

We'll now use the "How to Choose Just Three" and the "Reviews" exercises from Chapter 2 as background to create a storyboard—which is, very simply, a plan for the presentation. It outlines the agenda that you intend to cover during the presentation, the key points that you need to stress, and the stories and proof points that you want to include in each section. All of these are in the context of the *three key messages* that you have decided are most important to communicate to the client—the Big Three.

I recommend that the salesperson leading the team complete one overarching storyboard. Then each team member can create one for his or her particular section. This works very well—as it ensures that everyone is prepared for the strategy sessions and rehearsals leading up to the presentation.

Big Three Messages

1.
2.
3.

Topic	Critical Points	Opportunities to Reinforce the Big 3	Proof Points, Differentiators, Stories and Metaphors

The storyboard helps you organize your presentation by compelling you to focus on five key elements:

- The topics and the order in which you will present them (your agenda)
- The critical points within each of those topics
- The opportunities to reinforce your three key messages (the Big Three)
- The proof points and differentiators that can validate your points
- The stories and metaphors that will resonate with the audience and bring the presentation to life

The Topics and the Order in Which You Present Them

There's a common mistake that we often see in a company's standard presentation structure: It is organized in a way that makes sense to the company selling and how they think about their services instead of in a way that makes sense to how the prospective clients think about their needs. For example, there are some business-to-business industries (e.g., retirement services, health benefits, relocation services, and technology) in which the client typically has two overriding questions:

1. What will the experience of working with you be like for our employees?
2. What will the experience of working with you be like for those of us who are administering this service?

However, the sales organization is more apt to view their capabilities based on how they are organized. For example, they may think it makes sense to discuss their technology capabilities as a whole, because their technology department and the people presenting technology solutions to the client work on both. They may also be tempted to discuss communication to both employees and administrators together because their communications person is on the presentation team to discuss both. An agenda that's organized from the sales team's perspective is much more likely to appear disjointed and confusing to the client.

What happens when the client issues an agenda?

Often, before the sales presentation, a client will issue an agenda to the finalists presenting—for one of three reasons:

1. It is expected of them as part of the process.
2. They want to be certain that the sales team covers the material in which they are most interested.
3. They want to create a level playing field.

Most sales teams will follow the client's agenda diligently. However, I always encourage the salesperson to ask the client for permission to veer from the agenda. I suggest this because if all finalists approach the presentation the same way—and in the same order—it will be difficult for the sales team to stand out and provide a unique experience (note reason number 3). In fact, when procurement is involved, one of the roles that they often play is to get the vendors to look as much alike as possible so that the buying committee can base their decision on price.

We don't want to play this game. I therefore recommend that the salesperson call the client and say something like this: "Thanks for the agenda. We will make sure that we cover everything that you requested. We think that we can cover the material in a more meaningful and efficient way for you if we can change the order slightly. Assuming we cover everything that you have requested, would there be any problem if we reorganized the agenda slightly?"

I have found in most cases that clients agree, which automatically gives the salesperson requesting the exception a competitive advantage. If they do not agree, the salesperson obviously needs to follow the client's agenda and look for other opportunities in the introduction, transitions, and close to differentiate the experience. But it never hurts to ask, since there's only upside potential on this one—and it has proven to be well worth the phone call.

The Critical Points within Each Section

Similar to the concept of three critical points, a salesperson can request that each presenter identify three points they consider most important in their portion of the presentation. Again, they should be thinking in terms of:

- The client's needs
- Their own strengths
- The competitor's strengths and weaknesses

The Opportunities to Reinforce the Big Three Messages

Each presenter should also keep an eye out for opportunities to reinforce the Big Three messages. If, for example, one of the three messages is that "you will be a big fish in our small pond," one of the team members may draft a message that reinforces this by saying something along these lines: "Many of our clients appreciate the personal attention that we can give to them that larger organizations can't. For example, I had a client call me the other day, sounding quite nervous. She had just received notice that her company was going to be audited. I assured her we would be there, on-site, every step of the way through the process and that we had been through it many times. This is one of the benefits of working with an organization our size."

Proof Points

Proof points make promises real. They provide credibility and substance to claims that might initially sound like hot air. The best proof points are either quantitative or objective.

An example of a *quantitative* proof point is, "We were able to save the client 18 percent in one year by using this approach." Pow! Another is, "Client satisfaction increased from 76 percent to 93 percent." Bam! Quantitative proof points make a huge impact.

An *objective* proof point usually comes in the form of an award or a testimonial. Awards are great—flaunt them if you have them. Testimonials can be powerful as well; however, be sure to use them sparingly and creatively in a sales presentation.

Whether quantitative facts, awards, or testimonials, you always want to use proof points strategically to support the three critical messages.

Points of Differentiation

Buying committees are on a search for differentiation. They want to understand how one provider is unlike another. But the reality is that most of our offerings tend to mirror our competitors' offerings. Therefore, it's crucial that we point out any meaningful differences or decisive strengths very clearly to the client. Do not make clients search for them—and do not assume they will figure them out on their own.

When you have a clear advantage, point it out clearly to the client by saying something along the lines of the following examples:

"We are very proud of our call center's response time—in fact, I think you will find that this is a very clear differentiator from our competitors."

"This is a real strength for us and an area in which we are very different from our competitors."

Using words such as *differentiator*, *strength*, and *competitors* (without naming them) can really help to drive these points home.

Stories

Our job in the world of the complex sale is to eliminate (at least some of) the complexity for the client by providing a clear picture of our services and capabilities—as well as explaining how they will address the client's problems, needs, and opportunities. There is nothing more powerful than metaphors and stories to accomplish this.

There has been a lot of attention on storytelling in corporate America over the past several years. In fact, it is touted as so powerful that many forward-thinking companies like Pepsi, Microsoft, and Google are even providing storytelling workshops. The workshops often have participants first present concepts and information as they normally do, absent a story. They then give them a framework to develop a story around the concepts. Once the story has been crafted, each participant tells it to the group. The contrast between the two presentation styles results in an audience that truly understands the power of a story.

What makes stories so powerful? The answer to this is pretty obvious. I usually ask this very question when I conduct group workshops, and I have never had any problem getting a list of answers:

Stories are . . .

- Memorable
- Interesting
- Compelling

Because they . . .

- Make the intangible tangible
- Demonstrate success
- Foster personal connections
- Tap into people's emotions

These are all reasons to consider how and when to use stories in the presentation. I often suggest that people keep a log of key stories that they can incorporate into their presentation, as needed. I also suggest that sales organizations establish a process for sharing stories among the sales team. Section 2 of the book addresses the skills necessary for storytelling and provides some guidelines on the most effective way to tell a story.

Metaphors, Analogies, and Similes

Without getting hung up on the literary definitions of these terms, metaphors, analogies, and similes can be very powerful ways to explain parallel ideas to help a client understand and remember a concept, a capability, or a product's value or benefits. Used appropriately, they can also make a presentation more colorful and flavorful (two metaphors). Here are examples of how they can drive home important concepts:

"You will be able to sleep like a baby."
"We implement with surgical precision."
"We will serve as an extension of your HR department."

I have seen sales teams use analogies effectively when they relate the client's business to something that the company does. For example, a financial salesperson speaking to a pharmaceutical company might compare the rigor of a drug being approved by the FDA to the rigor of a complex financial product getting through compliance. An appropriate analogy is powerful as it can make an otherwise new or foreign concept familiar and relatable to a client.

The storyboard framework is designed to help you to craft a story that has all the important components:

- The three big messages
- Proof points and differentiators
- Stories within the bigger story
- Analogies, metaphors, and similes

It ultimately ensures that your presentation is succinct, clear, and memorable.

If You Remember Only Three Things:

1. Think about your presentation as a story. Before you open your PowerPoint, draft it out using a storyboard. Above all, make sure you're organizing it from the client's perspective (not yours).
2. If clients issue an agenda, don't automatically follow it. Seek permission to address the content that they want covered in a different way.
3. Have your Big Three messages drive your content and bring your presentation to life with proof points, stories, and metaphors.

Interview with Howard T. Owens

President, National Geographic Channels

After starting his entertainment career at global agency William Morris, Owens moved on to cofound Reveille LLC, a television and film production company with Ben Silverman. While at Reveille, he was the executive producer of television shows *Nashville Star* and *American Gladiator*, as well as coexecutive producer of *The Biggest Loser*. Owens was recently named president of National Geographic Channels—and has been on both the receiving and

(continued)

(*continued*)

giving ends of presentations in a business that is all about story-telling. Here's his take on storytelling:

> I have been pitched to by the best of them—including top television producers such as Ben Silverman, Mark Burnett, Dick Wolf and Lloyd Braun. It is mind-boggling how great these guys are at telling a story.
>
> Mark Burnett is really the best storyteller I have ever seen. He begins with a personal conversation that really connects with you, and then continues to tell a story that seems to grow organically.
>
> We are in the story business—so if someone comes in with charts and graphs, it is a "no-go." I want to hear a story that moves me, that is simple, yet has an exciting incident, some detail, an element of surprise. If I have to look at a PowerPoint or a binder, I'm done. While I have seen some effective uses of PowerPoint, and will use it myself when presenting to my board, it is always to illustrate the story or to prompt me. I never let it take over the conversation.
>
> You can't memorize your story. Burnett and Silverman never tell the same story; it is different every time. They take you on an emotional journey that underpins what they are selling. It always begins with an emotion—it might be self-deprecation, humor, or fear, but it is always an emotion.
>
> I don't want charts. I want to know people. I want to see the people behind everything. Don't give me a bunch of charts so that I feel like I am in 1995 again. Be current.
>
> Both stories and selling are about principals, not rules—it is about getting people excited and connecting with their emotions.

4

Developing Stories for Existing Clients (Rebids)

Tradition: Prepare for a rebid as you would any other sales presentation.

New tradition: Pull out all stops, and exploit your relationship.

An existing client going out to bid needs to be approached differently than a prospect. A rebid situation has both significant advantages and disadvantages—making it necessary for incumbents to leverage every advantage they have. Let's explore the disadvantages first; this way, we can recognize the hurdles right off the bat. In Chapter 3, we talked about the power of stories and metaphors. The following is a metaphorical story that illustrates the challenges and opportunities associated with rebids.

My husband Peter and I recently celebrated our twenty-second wedding anniversary. While I love him more than ever, our relationship now is certainly very different than it was during our courtship. We know each other much better than we did 20-plus years ago. We have shared our happiest, and saddest, days together and have celebrated our successes and failures together.

When we were first dating, I remember happily watching football next to him, and he would patiently shop with me. It is fairly obvious to both of us that those days are over. (I guess that's why they call it the honeymoon stage.)

Neither of us plans to rebid for a mate. However, if we were to do so, it would be hard for me to proclaim that I love watching football—and hard for him to praise the wonders of shopping. And there may be a few other habits and blemishes that neither one of us could deny.

That is the problem with a rebid.

Clients in these situations have come to know us intimately, warts and all, whereas competitors can arrive at the table with a shiny new penny—and with promises to watch football and go shopping.

However, what competitors cannot compete with is the intimate knowledge that you have of your clients and the successes that you have shared together. They don't know how your clients like their coffee, and they don't know what drives your clients crazy. It is therefore critical as an incumbent to capitalize on your knowledge and on the relationships that you have developed over time. These are things that will not be possible for competitors to replicate.

Be careful of those situations where it appears that clients are going to solicit bids only as part of their due diligence. Complacency is a kiss of death for incumbents in these scenarios. It is not enough to exhibit the same level of interest and desire for the business as the competitors do. Incumbents must show *more*. It's vital that they communicate to clients that they appreciate their business and desperately want to continue the relationship.

I recently coached a team who was presenting to a large law firm that had been an important client of theirs for a long time. The sales manager and the relationship manager knew that while the company had a long track record—and personally had a great relationship with the firm—they could not risk being, or even appearing to be, complacent. They had stiff competition, combined with a fly in the ointment, because the relationship manager (whom the client adored) had just been promoted and would be leaving the account. So, we had two issues to tackle:

1. How to demonstrate to the client our appreciation for their business and our desire to continue to work with them

2. How to tell them that the admired relationship manager was going off the account without sacrificing the deal

We brainstormed a bit on both issues. It was clear that we needed to focus on the history of the relationship, the intimate knowledge and insight that the team had developed about the client, and the personal relationships that they'd developed over time. We identified the Big Three messages:

1. We have a proven track record of results.
2. We "get" you (because we have been working with you for 20-plus years).
3. We value our relationship with you.

We conducted the Reviews Exercise, and uncovered the following emotions that we wanted to inspire in the client:

- "I like them too much to let them go."
- "We have too much history."
- "We'd have to start over with someone else."
- "We know we can trust them."

We knew it was critical that we communicate to the client's buying committee how important they were to us, that we valued them, and that we were not taking the relationship for granted. We brainstormed a little bit and realized that we needed to do something unusual and unexpected—something that would demonstrate our commitment to the relationship.

We decided to create a YouTube-like video that had each of the team members speaking from the heart about what the relationship meant to them. We strategized the best time to send it and decided that would be before the meeting. This would serve to warm up the buying committee by reminding them of the long-term relationship they had with the law firm. They would see the team's presentation the next day through the lens of familiarity and friendship.

The video was sent in an e-mail that read:

> Tomorrow's a big day for our team. When we see you, we will be presenting the business case to show why we remain your best choice in retirement plan providers.
>
> Of course, business isn't all about facts and figures; it's also about relationships. That's why the people who support you have recorded some personal messages in a brief video. Click here to view.
>
> See you tomorrow!

When the buying committee viewed the video, they were greeted first by the relationship manager:

> Before our meeting tomorrow, I and the rest of the team wanted to take a few minutes to thank you for the opportunity to reiterate our commitment to you. We know how important having the right partner is to you. And we know this is a big decision.
>
> One of the things that we are most proud of in our long relationship is that we have come to know you, your culture, and your preferences. And we know that it is important to you to have a provider that is, in essence, "smart in your world" [the client's slogan].

The relationship manager continued for about 30 seconds, citing examples of specific servicing preferences that they had. After her opening, each team member told a personal story that demonstrated his or her intimate knowledge of the relationship. Each segment was a minute or less and ended with the the client's slogan "We're smart in your world."

One of the buying committee members, a senior partner at the firm, was known to be a Shakespeare buff. Over the years, he had shared his interest with one of the team members who had been an English teacher early in his career and also had an interest in

Shakespeare. This is a great example of how personal interests can build strong connections between businesspeople. He ended his section of the video by stating, "As Shakespeare wrote, 'in such business, action is eloquence,' so I look forward to being active and smart in your world."

The video concluded with a brief statement of commitment from the company president.

I understand the buying committee was very appreciative of the video when they met the next morning.

As I mentioned, the beloved (and I'm not exaggerating here!) relationship manager was going off the account. Of course, this couldn't have been worse timing. Although it would have been tempting to deliver this news after the decision, the team knew that the only right thing to do was to provide full disclosure in advance of the finals presentation—especially since one of the key emotions they wanted to inspire was trust. So the relationship manager called each of her key contacts at the law firm to give them the news. She discussed their new coverage model and promised that she would be involved throughout the transition. The new relationship manager would attend the finals. We made sure he had a lead role so that the client could get a sense of what it would be like to work with him going forward.

The law firm must have been convinced that the new coverage model would not compromise their service and that the relationship was well worth continuing. The sales team was able to retain the business—much to the delight of everyone involved.

It is estimated that it costs five times more to obtain a new client than to keep an existing one. We also know that existing clients tend to be much more profitable than new ones. Of course, the costs associated with a loss go way beyond the direct revenue when you consider the potential impact on market perception—something that's very difficult to quantify.

This is a great example of a sales team and organization that understands the value of an existing relationship. Not only were they willing to invest in the time and resources, they were also creative in their approach, which resulted in a win for everyone.

Tips for Rebids

1. Do not take any relationship for granted—no matter how good it is.
2. Understand your advantages and disadvantages:
   - *Advantage*: You know them better than anyone else.
   - *Advantage*: You have developed (hopefully) intimate personal relationships.
   - *Advantage*: Unless you have really screwed up, you will be considered the safer choice.
   - *Advantage*: Depending on the industry, it can be a nightmare to transition.
   - *Disadvantage*: They have seen your warts and flaws.
   - *Disadvantage*: Talented competitors can promise the world, and your client just may be tempted to believe it.
3. Exploit your advantages to the hilt!
4. Take the time to strategize ways that you can demonstrate your commitment and your appreciation (ideally, you have been doing this all along).

If You Remember Only Three Things:

1. Do not be complacent with rebids—clients expect more of you!
2. Exploit the history of the relationship and the insight that you have gained.
3. Find creative ways to show your appreciation for their business and your desire to continue the relationship.

The Skill: How You Say It

5 Facilitating the Experience

Myth: Facilitation happens naturally.
Truth: Facilitation must be carefully planned and orchestrated.

There should always be one person responsible for facilitating the sales presentation. While this is typically the salesperson, it can be particularly powerful to assign this role to the person who will hold the responsibility for the day-to-day relationship. This allows this person to build credibility, to demonstrate the ability to manage a process, and to show his or her commitment to addressing the clients' needs and what is important to them.

It's especially crucial to take this approach in a rebid situation, where a relationship with an account manager or a relationship manager already exists. Handing over the reigns to a salesperson (assuming he or she does not have a relationship with the client) can cheapen the tone of the meeting. It can also potentially make clients feel like they are being sold to, which is the last thing you want. Ideally, they should feel as though they're choosing to extend the existing relationship as a natural course of business.

Facilitation skills are paramount to the sales presentation's effectiveness. The facilitator's role is a complex one that requires a great deal of confidence, presence, and organization. Facilitators often have to think on their feet in situations where every detail has not gone exactly as planned (which is almost always the case).

The facilitator is responsible for managing each section of the presentation, including:

- The opening
- The introductions
- The agenda
- Reviewing and confirming the understanding of needs
- Transitions
- Questions and answers
- The close

The facilitator also:

- Sets the tone
- Manages the time
- Checks in with the buying committee to ensure understanding
- Elicits feedback and makes the appropriate adjustments on the fly

The primary skills required for effective facilitation are:

- Questioning
- Listening
- Paraphrasing
- Summarizing

It is an understatement to say that there's a significant burden on facilitators. Fortunately, they can usually share this burden with other team members by delegating some of the responsibility. For example, I always suggest that the facilitator assign a fellow team member with the responsibility for tracking time. If this individual notices that they are running overtime according to the schedule that was agreed upon in the rehearsal, he or she can signal the facilitator. If the facilitator does not see the signal, the backup timekeeper has permission to say something like this: "Kristin, I have noticed that we have 20 minutes left; perhaps we should check in with everyone." The facilitator would then say something like, "Thanks, Maggie—great idea. This has been a terrific discussion, and we could talk about our client service all day. I'd like to take a moment to review with you what we have left on the agenda and ask you how you would like to allocate the time remaining."

Similarly, it's a good idea for one person on the team to take backup responsibility for assuring that the team has addressed the objectives that were mentioned in the client introductions. As such, that person has permission to say something like this: "Ray, I know this was of particular importance to you. Has Maggie addressed your questions?"

I usually ask this person to take on an additional responsibility—paying close attention to the buying committee's body language. Folded arms, confused or puzzled looks, dazed or bored expressions, and/or BlackBerry and wristwatch checking might indicate the need to check in with the audience. The person assigned this responsibility has permission to interject something like, "Meredith, it looks like you have a question or something you would like to say." Or this person may say to the facilitator, "Kristin, there may be some questions here. Why don't we check in with the group?"

These types of redirections require a great deal of trust between the facilitator and the rest of the team. Team members also need some finesse to uphold the facilitator's credibility during these exchanges. There's less risk of compromising credibility if the team members defer to the facilitator instead of taking over themselves. When orchestrated effectively, this approach can send a strong signal to the client that you work well as a team.

The facilitator can also delegate the role of scribing. While I prefer that the facilitator do his or her own scribing in order to maintain full control, I understand that some people either have not developed this skill or simply do not have readable handwriting. In this case, go ahead and delegate it (but practice and develop your scribing skills internally for future presentations!).

Facilitating the introductions is one of the first and most important parts of the process, as it sets the tone for the entire meeting.

Tradition: Introduce yourself by stating your name, title and number of years you have been with the company and/or in the industry.

New tradition: Introduce yourself by stating what you will do for the client, while bringing your most likable self to the table.

"Between us we have 826 and a half years of experience."

A traditional introduction in a sales presentation usually sounds something like this: "Hi, my name is Christopher Bennett, and I am the Assistant Associate Director of Communications. I have been with Acme, Inc., for more than 12 years, and I've worked in the industry for 18 years. I'm happy to be here today."

Then, pleased that he is finished, he looks to the team member who will provide another equally boring introduction that is likely to be just as meaningless to the client: "Hi, I am PK Isacs, and I am an Associate Regional Manager of Development. I have been with Acme for three years. Prior to this, I was at [blah, blah, blah, blah, blah . . .]." And on and on and on.

This format has been around forever—so much so that it is almost expected. The truth, however, is that clients usually forget your name, have no idea what your title means, and (assuming that you look older than 21) could care less about the number of years you have been anywhere.

It is ironic that the introductions component of the sales presentation—traditionally, the most painful part—is usually also the most important. It sets the tone and the personality of the meeting and helps the buying team assess whether they want to work with you. They are consciously or unconsciously asking the question, "Do I like these people?"

PET PEEVE

I can't tell you how many times I have witnessed a salesperson summarize his or her teammates' introductions by saying something like, "Between us, we have 124 years of experience in the room."

What does this mean? Who cares? If the competitor team has 143 years of experience, does that mean they are the better choice? I don't think so. And neither does the client.

Of all the potential messages that a salesperson could convey, is this the strongest? Of course not. But again, we tend to do these things because that is what we saw our predecessors do.

We have all heard the adage that "all things being equal, people buy from people that they like." I would go so far as to say that even when things aren't so equal, people buy from people they like. In fact, I have been one of those buyers looking for every reason to work with someone I like. Haven't you? In many cases, after the sale, we are going to be talking to these people on a weekly—if not daily—basis. Depending on the scenario, we may be in war rooms together for long hours working on complex projects, possibly sharing meals together, and perhaps even traveling together. Who wants to spend this much time with someone you don't like?

I recall a recent situation where I met a young woman outside a conference room before the rest of the deal team arrived for a rehearsal. We chatted for about 10 minutes, discussing the deal as well as her upcoming wedding. I was struck by her open smile and her sense of humor as she laughed about going dress shopping with her brides-maids. When the rest of the team arrived, we all gathered around the conference table and I conducted a quick warm-up. When it was time for my new friend to speak, it seemed as if she had been replaced by her Stepford twin—either that or she had left her smile and sense of humor outside with the coffee. She became a completely different—and much less animated—person in this professional environment.

Why is it that we so often leave our likable selves outside the boardroom door? Possibly, it's one of a number of reasons:

- *The environment tends to be more formal.* Boardrooms can be intimidating and sterile environments, and our behavior tends to mirror the atmosphere. While, of course, we want to be professional and have an appropriate demeanor, we don't want to be so formal that we lose our true personality.
- *There is a lot at stake!* Let's face it: This is the make-or-break sit-uation; this is where the rubber meets the road; this is the moment of truth. However you want to describe it, it's a very intimidating situation for people. At this point, your team has invested a great deal of time, effort, and expense—and this is the point at which it all comes to fruition, so you better not screw it up!
- *We usually tend to focus on the script.* "I have to remember to say X and to not stray from this." This kind of preoccupation with the facts and figures may get in the way of our ability to be in the present moments and to connect with the people in the room.

- *Nerves can get the best of us.* A common symptom of being nervous is to withdraw and become a smaller version of ourselves.
- *There is confusion between being professional and being robotic.* We often say to ourselves, "This is a very serious subject; therefore, I need to be very serious and all about business."

Now that we have explored some of the obstacles that may hinder your ability to showcase your fantastic personality, let's look at ways that you can make your introductions compelling and get the client excited about the potential of working with you.

Seven Guidelines for Powerful Introductions:

1. *Forget the titles!* Instead of stating your title, tell clients what you will do for them. For example, "I am the person who will be responsible for making sure that all of your employees are up to speed on the new system," or, "My role is to manage your transition. I'll ensure that all deadlines are met and that the transition goes as smoothly and seamlessly as possible."
2. *Incorporate emotion.* Don't be afraid to tell clients what you like about your job and how happy you are to be helping them. Hearing your enthusiasm will only make them pleased. You can say things like, "What I love most about what I do is . . ." or, "I am very excited to be here today because . . ."
3. *Leave the corporate mask at home. Show your personality!* It could be as simple as a smile or as bold as incorporating humor. And let clients know if you have a connection with them or their products in some way. This will build rapport and give you an immediate edge. For example,
   Presenting to Stop & Shop: "My first job was working at a grocery store."
   Presenting to Mars: "I have a personal addiction to M&Ms."
   Presenting to Starwood Hotels: "Your hotels are so comfortable to me that we actually purchased a W bed last year."

4. *Practice, practice, practice.* We spend a good amount of time practicing the introductions when we coach teams to prepare for a presentation. I typically suggest that all team members spend a few minutes on their own, drafting an introduction that will accomplish these objectives:
   - Showing their personality
   - Establishing their credibility

   After each person has written down his or her intro, we practice and give each other feedback. It is most effective when the introductions go in order of the seating; after one person finishes his or her introduction, that individual hands it to a teammate by looking at the teammate and saying the person's name (e.g., "Jane . . ."). Though it seems minor, this gesture can send a message of camaraderie to clients and let them know how well you work as a team.

   It's often the case in presentations that some people will have a bigger role than others. As such, I allocate a little more of the introduction time to those who will have less time in the presentation.

5. *Replace number of years with relevant experience.* Your accomplishments and experience with similar clients in the same or similar industries have a greater impact than the numbers of years you have been in the industry or with your firm. Highlight successes you have had that are likely to resonate with the client. For example, you might say, "I have had the opportunity to work with several clients in your industry and am very familiar with the unique needs of your diverse workforce. In fact, our work in your industry has been nationally recognized."

6. *Bring your authentic self to the table.* Be you. If you are not particularly outgoing, don't try to be in this situation. If you have a sense of humor, don't hold it back, but don't try to tell jokes if you aren't much of a jokester. Bottom line: Know thyself. But try to connect. Eye contact and a smile go a long way in establishing rapport.

7. *Be creative!* Introductions can present an opportunity to stand out from your competition, create a positive climate for the meeting, and demonstrate your desire to win the business.

I recently coached a team that was presenting to packaged food company ConAgra. Because ConAgra employees have a tagline on their e-mail that states their favorite ConAgra product, we decided to incorporate this idea in the introductions.

After introducing themselves and what they do, each sales team member cited their favorite ConAgra product and told the buying committee what made it special to them. They physically brought the product to the presentation so that the team member could take it out from under the table and place it in front of them during each introduction. One member, whose favorite product was Jiffy Pop popcorn, explained that he has young children and that in his house, every Saturday night is movie night—which just wouldn't be complete without the Jiffy Pop!

Another told of her childhood memories with Reddi-wip—and her mother's distain for her children's habit of squirting the Reddi-wip straight from the can into their mouths, which, of course, only made them do it more frequently.

When it came time for the buying committee to introduce themselves, they did the same—without even being asked (and, of course, without the props). As a result, members of both groups made some pretty significant personal connections. Personalities were highlighted, a few laughs were had, and a positive climate for the meeting was set.

When we debriefed after the presentation, the team said that the connection that they fostered with the buying committee was so strong that the client team members actually hugged them on the way out the door. Honestly—they hugged them! They attributed this connection largely to the tone set during the introductions.

I recently coached a team that was presenting to the City of San Francisco. The salespeople decided to share their favorite thing about the city. One talked about his first trip to San Francisco as a young child and his fascination with trolley cars; another discussed her fondness for sourdough bread; another talked about his favorite movie, *The Rock*, and shared that he could not leave the city this time without a visit to Alcatraz. Once again, the buying committee had an opportunity to see the sales team as real people to whom they could relate. In fact, one committee member spurred by the Alcatraz story told the group during his introduction that his brother had actually been an extra in the movie. After the presentation, he pulled the Alcatraz fan aside to tell him that he had some interesting behind-the-scenes stories to share with him at a later time.

So, how do these guidelines actually play out? Here is an example.

AN EXAMPLE OF A POWERFUL INTRODUCTION

Good Morning.

I am Melinda Hammer, and I will to be your go-to person on the entire relationship—which means I am responsible for coordinating the timely and efficient delivery of our capabilities. One of my favorite things about what I do is being your advocate within our firm. This means that I will get to know you inside and out—and essentially become an extension of your organization.

I must tell you that I was so thrilled to learn about the potential opportunity to work with you, because I have admired your company for a long time—particularly your commitment to work–life balance. As a working mother of three, I know just how important this is.

Later in the meeting, I look forward to talking a little bit more about my role in helping you meet your objectives.

David? [She turns it over to the next person.]

Notice in this example that Melinda did not mention her title or her years or experience; instead, she talked about what her role is in servicing the client. By saying what she loves about what she does she brings a spirit of enthusiasm to the table—along with a little insight into who she is as a professional. The members of the client team are likely to feel complimented by her stated admiration for the company, and they get to see a little glimpse of the human side of her when she mentions that she has three children.

In case you are wondering—when timed, this introduction took all of 52 seconds to deliver. I typically estimate about one minute per person, and I know that it's well worth the time investment.

Client Introductions

Tradition: Let clients introduce themselves the way they want to.
New tradition: Facilitate client introductions by telling them how you would like them to introduce themselves.

Typically, after the sales team has introduced themselves, they hand the floor over to the client to do the same. Most often, the members of the client team will provide their names and titles—then the business of the meeting will begin.

A sales team that follows this common, run-of-the-mill pattern loses an opportunity to gain valuable insight into what is important to each individual on the buying committee. In the case where your team is presenting after the competition, you have also lost the opportunity to uncover hints on what the clients have learned from the earlier presentations—and how this may have influenced their thinking.

To capture and fully leverage these opportunities, we suggest that the facilitator lead the client's introductions after the sales team's introductions by saying something like this: "Okay—so that is our team. We'd now like to ask you to introduce yourselves. If you would please share your name, your area of responsibility, and—because each of you wears a different hat and has a different perspective—we will also ask you to tell us what you personally would like to get out of today's meeting."

We often suggest that the facilitator write down each person's response on a flip chart. At the end of the presentation (but before the close), he or she can refer back to the comments to ensure that the team has addressed each request. This sends a very strong message to clients that this meeting is about them and will focus entirely on how you will help them meet their needs.

Eric Baron, president of The Baron Group, says that treating introductions this way allows you to change what feels like a one-on-five presentation (one person presenting to however many are on the client's team) to what feels like a one-on-one presentation by connecting what you are presenting to the interests of each individual. For example, a presenter may say, "George, you said in your introduction that you were particularly interested in knowing how we evaluate our call center representatives." This speaks to this person's specific need—and lets that individual know that you were listening.

Many years ago, I had an opportunity to coach a team on a high-stakes deal. The team had just participated in a consultative selling program and bought into the idea of handling introductions this way. In fact, they had even practiced it. Yet when it came time to plan out the agenda, there was quite a bit of pushback on the introductions. It came in the form of, "I get why this makes sense, but we have only an hour and a half for this meeting; we couldn't possibly take this much time for introductions."

We negotiated back and forth a bit. I reminded them that getting the client talking early in the presentation sets the tone, that they could uncover critical information that might help them determine what's on the buying committee members' minds, and, most important, that we had to make this presentation about them and that this was one way to do so. Eventually, they succumbed.

While conducting a debrief after their presentation, one of the team members said: "If we win this deal, the reason will be because we handled introductions the way you suggested. There was a consultant in the room who had had a bad experience with a previous transition we had done, and he said so in his introductions.

He said something to the effect that 'to be honest with you, one of my other clients went with you guys and it was a very lengthy and complicated transition. Your systems were a mess. I want to know what you have done about it.'"

Yikes! Who wants to hear that at the beginning of a presentation? The salesperson went on to say, "Had we not asked each of them to share what they were interested in, the consultant probably would have waited until we were gone to voice his concern—and we would not have been able to address it. In fact, we were planning to skim over the transition because it was the last thing mentioned on their agenda—and therefore did not seem like a hot button for them. Instead, we were able to address the issue up front by telling them about the new Six Sigma approach we've implemented, our investment in technology, and our high customer ratings since instituting it."

I am happy to report that they won the deal. And I take great comfort in knowing that for as long as this team is conducting sales presentations, they will facilitate introductions this way, because they had an opportunity to experience the success of the approach. Like so many other teams we coach, they had initially resisted the suggested approach. The pushback, usually centered on time issues, sounds something like this: "I have six people on my team, and there are six people on the client's team. This means that introductions will take almost 15 minutes—and we only have an hour!! I can't take 25 percent of the meeting time for this!"

Trust me, I hear you. However, I want to remind you of the following:

- The sales presentation is about the people in the room and the connections they make. Your sales team's introductions allow you to set that tone, establish your personality, and connect with everyone at the table as people.
- Taking time to elicit what is on the minds of the buying committee members results in a competitive advantage. The more you know about what's going on in their heads, the better.

- Asking the buying committee what is important to them—and then addressing it—demonstrates your commitment to meeting the client's needs through your behavior (the strongest proof point that there is).

While it may be tempting to shorten the introductions and allocate that time elsewhere, I assure you that it's well worth protecting the time in the agenda.

If You Remember Only Three Things:

1. Facilitation is a critical skill that will impact the success of every sales presentation, so carefully plan out the facilitation for each presentation.
2. Introductions are an opportunity to showcase your personalities and what you will be like to work with. Clients don't care about your titles—they care about what you will do for them.
3. Client introductions are an opportunity to gain critical insight into the current thinking of the buying committee, as well as a chance to demonstrate that this meeting will be all about them.

CHALLENGE

Practice and strategize introductions for your next sales presentation.

Interview with a Partner in a Private Equity Firm

The following is an interview with a partner in a private equity firm who has asked to remain anonymous. His firm manages more than $3 billion on behalf of corporate pension plans, public retirement systems, university endowment funds, and the executives of the firm's portfolio companies. He is commonly on the receiving end of many presentations designed to compel him and his partners to invest.

Here he shares his pet peeve:

> My biggest pet peeve is when [the person presenting doesn't tell or] show me the full story up front. Don't try to hook me and then give me the bad news later. For example, I had a manufacturer who was presenting information about customer concentration. They had cut the numbers in such a way that they suggested they have more clients than they do (by counting each division of Walmart separately). When I found out the real numbers (after flying to Chicago to meet them), I wanted to take a baseball bat and smash their projector! We walked away [from the deal]. Even if we could have lived with the numbers, there was no trust.
>
> Another thing that drives me crazy is when there is no data to back up assertions. If someone makes a statement—I want to know that there is data behind it.
>
> When I talk about my fund, I always try to be as transparent as possible and then talk about the mitigating factors. Honesty and trustworthiness are paramount. We can have five investment bankers in here in a row [who] all tell us that they are number one in the league tables. What is that all about?

And he offers three pieces of advice:

> When I coach my management team to give a presentation, I want to make sure that every slide has a point and
>
> (*continued*)

(continued)

a conclusion. When investment bankers show me their org chart, I often feel like saying, "I never doubted that you had an organization." I'm never sure what the point of this slide is . . . but they all have it!

I remember telling a colleague once that presenting is about telling a story. He had an interesting response: "I don't want to tell a story; I want to tell the truth." But a story is not a lie; it is a string of facts woven together in a compelling and interesting way.

Don't overrehearse your presenters. [We once had] a couple of businessmen in here from China who had moved to the United States and were pitching us their business. It was pretty clear that the investment banker had coached them on their script. Throughout the presentation they were required to say, "mom and pop." It was clear they were not familiar with the expression, as they kept saying "mop and pop." While it is important to be prepared, don't lose yourself in the process—you need to be genuine and show who you are.

6 Speaking the Client's Language

Tradition: Speak in tongues.
Breaking tradition: Speak in plain old English.

I began working at Chase Bank when I was 23 years old. It was my second job. I had been a liberal arts major in college and was coming from what I thought was a very glamorous job in Washington, DC, working for a trade association.

All was good in the world when I was in DC, with one exception: I wanted to be living and working in New York City. A colleague put me in touch with a headhunter who said that she could envision me at either Citibank or Chase. I couldn't imagine what she was thinking at the time; the last place I could ever see myself working was a bank! At the time, I'm not sure I had ever successfully balanced my checkbook, let alone read a spreadsheet. But I went along with it because I was desperate to move to New York.

I had 11 (yes, 11) interviews for my $40,000-a-year job. I was interviewing for a position in a special training function that reported directly to the vice chairman. The mandate was to turn the commercial bankers into investment bankers by training them in areas such as corporate finance, capital markets, risk management, and so forth.

The entry-level position for which I was interviewing was called "training designer," and my title would be "assistant treasurer."

While I hadn't a clue what that meant (and was afraid to ask), the position sounded appealing; there seemed to be a creative element to it, sort of like an interior designer or a fashion designer. The title, however, was just plain scary . . . assistant treasurer? What was that?

For almost the entire first year in my new position, I had no idea what anyone was talking about. It seemed as though I could understand only about every fifth word. I knew that my employers wanted to "leverage the core competencies" and that they needed "intellectual capital" so that they could "move story paper" rather than "plain-vanilla products." I knew no one wanted the "junk" and that "LBOs" were big and important, although I did not know what the "drivers" were.

A couple of months into the job, I remember very clearly waking up in the middle of the night in a panic, thinking, "I have no idea what anyone is saying!" Well, somehow I managed, and as the years went by I found that I could sling jargon with the best of them (while not even aware I was doing so).

Twenty-five years later, I can't help but wonder how many people in corporate America do not understand each other.

It's a given that every industry and business will have some level of jargon. But some organizations are bigger culprits than others at overusing these industry- and company-specific words and phrases. It is so ingrained in most corporate cultures that we sometimes do not recognize jargon when we hear it.

Acronyms, for instance, are always jargon—and some organizations have created their very own language using acronyms. In fact, I have a client whose name is a six-letter acronym! It took me several days to get to a point where it just rolled off my tongue. And, of course, everyone's job title in the company is shrunk to an acronym, as are most product names. To an outsider, listening to a basic conversation in that organization is like listening to code.

Job titles are jargon, which is why I suggested in Chapter 5 that they be dropped from the introductions. Recently, while working with a client, I asked about a title in the form of an acronym that was being tossed back and forth throughout the meeting. When I asked what it stood for, the group hesitated, offered a couple of possibilities, and then laughed—as they realized that even they did not know.

I wonder how much time we save when using acronyms. How many seconds do we save by saying *AE* rather than *account executive* or *RM* rather than *relationship manager*? I hope we are using all that extra time wisely! Sometimes I think that people use jargon so they feel "in the know," which implies that there is a group that is "out of the know." This, of course, is typically not a good thing—particularly if that group includes your clients!

Product names are also jargon—and while there are some exceptions, these names typically do not describe what the product does. Yet this, of course, is what is most important to the client. Product names tend to become so ingrained in company culture that the people who use them forget that the rest of the world has never heard them before.

A series of words and phrases has crept into corporate America that I consider jargon as well—words and phrases that I consider meaningless. In some cases, they have lost their meaning from pure overuse; in other cases, they never meant much in the first place. Either way, using them in a sales presentation can have the same impact as the voice of Charlie Brown's teacher in *Peanuts*. Remember her? "Wa wa wa wa wa."

Here are examples of some of my favorite meaningless words and phrases:

- Trusted financial advisor
- Thought leader
- Change agent
- Best practices
- Strategic alliance

Each industry and specialty has its own collection of jargon. And, of course, there is also generational jargon (when my teenage boys say something is "dirty," I assume I need to do laundry—go figure).

We must remember that buying committees are often composed of people of varying backgrounds and expertise. They often include a combination of both generalists and specialists, some of whom can be highly technical. Everyone in the room needs to be able to understand our language, regardless of their background, technical specialty, or age. Clients do not have time to learn our language, nor should they have to. The last place that our jargon and acronyms belong is in a sales presentation.

Research suggests that perceived trustworthiness increases when salespeople use plain language. Conversely, communicators who give presentations laden with jargon are not well received—mostly because the audience simply doesn't understand what they are talking about. This can cause clients to feel suspicious about the information being presented. When plain language is used it allows the audience to better understand and validate the information on their own. It makes both the message and the speaker more credible.

However, editing the jargon can be challenging. These words are so embedded in industry and company cultures that it is often hard to distinguish jargon from plain ol' English. A good place to start is by looking at your product names—because you're likely to find that most are jargon. Encourage your salespeople to describe the product in terms of what it does rather than by its name. If they must use the product name, make sure that they define it clearly. For example, "We have a very powerful tool that will help you to track your pipeline so that you can see the status of every deal and can better forecast your sales results. We call this Deal Tracker." Or, "I am going to tell you about a product we call Deal Tracker; this will help you track your pipeline, allow you to see the status of every deal, and better forecast sales results."

Once you are conscious of your product names as jargon, scour your presentation for acronyms and remove them from all your presentation materials and notes. I also encourage people to stop using them internally so that they will be less likely to use them with clients. Finally, take a fresh look at those terms and expressions that people outside of your industry would not understand.

CHALLENGE

Review your last presentation and notes while pretending that it's your first day on the job. What words and acronyms would you not understand?

Another option: Give your presentation to someone outside of your industry—perhaps a spouse, a family member, or a trusted client. Ask that person to take note of words that he or she does not understand.

Emotion and Power Words

Put yourself in a client's shoes. You critically need to have something done by year-end, and you ask the sales team "Can you have this completed by December?" Which response will give you more confidence: "We absolutely can," or, "Yes, we can"? If you answered the former, you are absolutely right.

While we do not want salespeople and team members to get hung up on delivering a word-by-word script in a presentation, we do want them to be conscious of the impact of words and use them strategically. I suggest that people write out what they want to say and how they want to say it, because this will compel them to think strategically about the words that are likely to have the greatest impact on the audience. Writing these down in advance—and then reading over the script a few times—will increase the likelihood that these important words will come to them when they need them.

There are two types of words to consider here: (1) words that foster emotion and (2) words that communicate power. For instance— *excited*, *enthused*, and *concerned* are all emotion words, whereas terms like *critical*, *definitely*, and *positively* all convey power. An audience that hears "The following factors are critically important" is more likely to pay close attention to what the speaker is about to say.

Likewise, "a very powerful model for changing behavior" is much more convincing than "a great model," or "an effective model."

Following is a list of words that convey power and emotion. I often have people think about the words that they want to use as they are creating their storyboards.

Power Words	Emotional Words
Absolutely	Excited
Critical	Delighted
Essential	Love
Ultimate	Amazing
Authentic	Astonishing
Tested	Hate
Powerful	Passionate
Revolutionary	Fear
Strong	Happy
Convinced	Trust
Certain	Concerned

Similarly, certain phrases convey power and conviction.

- *Demonstrated value*
- *Critically important*
- *Guaranteed results*
- *Proven outcomes*

Finally, there are a couple of stage-setting, attention-grabbing clauses that will get clients pumped up:

- "One thing that our clients really appreciate when working with us is . . ."
- "Something that we are particularly proud of is . . ."
- "A powerful differentiator for us is . . ."
- "You will find that we really stand out when it comes to . . ."

CHALLENGE

Select one or two of these words and phrases and consciously use them over the next several days. Make an effort to incorporate them into your next sales presentation.

The Most Powerful Word in Sales: *You*

It is hard to believe this little pronoun holds as much power as I claim—but it does. In fact, some psychologists suggest that it is the most powerful word in the human language. This is based on the premise that people are most interested in themselves—a premise upon which this book is essentially based as well. I know the concept can seem quite unappealing, since most of us like to think that we are more altruistic than the assertion suggests, but a great deal of research supports it, as well as common sense. Nothing is more stimulating or interesting to us than our own interests, beliefs, goals, and desires. For our entire existence, we have focused on this; it is, in some respects, all that we really have.

No one is more aware of this than marketers who write copy for advertisements. They understand the power of the word *you* and use it every day. They know that when people are presented with two like propositions, one of which contains the word *you* and one that does not, people will be more favorably inclined to respond to the one containing the word *you*. For example, read the following two statements:

1. Salespeople can benefit from using powerful and emotional language in their sales presentations.
2. You will benefit from using powerful and emotional language in your sales presentations.

Do you find yourself more attracted to the second one? If you are like most people, you do.

CHALLENGE

Review your standard presentation and analyze how many times you use the word *you*. Look for opportunities to incorporate it more often.

When Numbers Count

Just as word choice is important, numbers—and the way that you use them—can have a significant, positive impact on a sales presentation's effectiveness. I am not talking about a slide filled with data that no one can interpret; we have all seen those. I am talking about strategically using numbers to get an audience's attention and to provide credibility to our messages.

Two Reasons to Use Numbers

1. *Numbers are attention grabbers.* When used correctly, numbers can play an important role in getting an audience's attention. Recall that we discussed the power of the number three in Chapter 1, which is why I end every chapter with a feature called "If You Remember Only Three Things." While three is certainly a magic number (for all the reasons previously discussed), other low numbers can be powerful as well—particularly when you use them to begin or end a section of your sales presentation. When your lead-in or close contains a number, it grabs the audience's attention and helps them to focus. For example,
   - "If there is one idea that I think warrants your attention . . ."
   - "I will review four steps with you today."

- "The two most critical aspects of a technology strategy are . . ."
- "The three secrets to our success with clients like you . . ."

2. *Numbers imply credibility.* Numbers make people believe that your statements are grounded in something concrete and real. The next time you're at a newsstand, notice how many magazine covers promote articles that have a number in the title: "The five secrets to happiness," "The six steps to successful weight loss," "The 100 most beautiful people."

Magazines use such titles because numbers make the information seem more credible. Since numbers themselves are not subjective, we assume that whatever they are attached to is also concrete. If you have a process, technique, or methodology that you review in your sales process, consider labeling it with a number. For example,

- Our five-step process
- The three pillars of client service
- Eight steps to a seamless transition

Years ago, I knew a consultant who was a pro at using numbers to boost his credibility. He would back up almost every assertion he made with a number: "The most important thing that you can do to increase revenues is to identify a select number of key accounts and develop those relationships. In fact, you can increase your revenues by as much as 28 percent in one year."

He would then continue by saying something like, "When asked, 22 percent of clients say that their relationship manager does not understand their needs, whereas 78 percent of relationship mangers say that they do understand their clients' needs."

This individual captured the audience's attention and wowed them with his knowledge. And the numbers seemed particularly credible because they were not round numbers—28 percent (not 30 percent), 22 percent (not 20 percent). Round numbers and those that end in a five seem too perfect to be real, and they sometimes feel manufactured.

I was recently reviewing a presentation with a team that I was coaching, when we came to a slide about client satisfaction research. The headline, which displayed a vertical scale, read, "Percentage of very satisfied employees." This team's name was at the top—and next to it was "48 percent." I thought to myself, am I reading this right? Less than half of the employees are satisfied. Is this supposed to be good news? I assumed that there must be something wrong, so I asked the team about it. They explained to me that while the percentage sounds low, it is in fact high in their industry. They went on to inform me that they're ranked higher than their competitors. In fact, this slide was meant to illustrate just how much higher their ratings were than those of their competitors. Unfortunately, it didn't accomplish this, because three issues were at play:

1. *Context.* It is possible that this buying committee would not know what typical employee satisfaction rates are in the industry—it is unlikely that the competition would be advertising their lower rankings! So it is quite possible that a ranking of 48 percent would seem pretty dismal to most observers (as it certainly did to me!).
2. *Consistency.* The headline on the slide was inconsistent with the message. The real message was that they outranked their peers in employee satisfaction.
3. *Complexity.* While the person presenting the slide may have explained everything in a favorable way, the chances of the client actually hearing that person's message were quite low. Anyone watching this would likely be more focused on trying to figure out the numbers represented on the scale than on listening to the presenter.

It was unclear whether there was a "satisfied" number that could be added to the "very satisfied" number to help with the optics, since we did not have the actual research or the time to go get it. So the first question I asked was, "Is the data that we have compelling?" We decided that it was, because they were significantly ahead of their competition, and this was something that the client had previously cited as important. The next step was to figure out a way to express it to make it compelling to the client. We did the math and found that the ranking was 33 percent higher than the top competitor's ranking. Since 33 percent is actually a lower number than 48 percent we needed to be very careful to provide the right context. We came up with with a slide headline that read, "Highest client satisfaction in the industry!"—and added, in a large font, "33 percent higher!" The scale was left as background.

It is not uncommon to find similar slides in presentations—those with data that do not make sense or are not consistent with the intended message. This is why you and your sales team must review these slides very carefully and with an objective eye. Here are some guidelines to keep in mind:

- *Be sure to present context.* Some numbers that may appear positive to you may not seem so to your clients—particularly when the numbers drop below 90 percent.
- *Strategize whether to use whole numbers or percentages.* Have you ever noticed "four out of five dentists recommend sugarless gum for their patients who chew gum?" Why not 80 percent of dentists? Because 80 percent makes it feel less compelling: It spurs me to think of a group of 20 dentists who do *not* recommend it. Yet when I hear four out of five, I am thinking that the four dentists are clearly in the majority and that there is just one dentist (probably nerdy and uptight) who is opposed, so I will go for the sugarless gum.
- *Work with the numbers, so that they send the message you want them to send.* Consider, for example, adding two numbers together (number of satisfied and very satisfied customers) to create a larger, more appealing number.

- *Present only the numbers that support your point.* Too many numbers can be confusing and dilute the message that you are trying to convey.

CHALLENGE

Review your presentation for numbers by asking yourself:

- Where can I use them to provide extra credibility when introducing a process or method?
- How can I present them so that they are most compelling?
- What context does the slide need?
- What is needed on this slide? Can I edit some numbers?
- Does the headline clearly communicate the message?

If You Remember Only Three Things:

1. Drop the jargon from your presentation. Pay close attention to product names, acronyms, and meaningless phrases that have crept into your day-to-day vernacular.
2. Use emotion and power words, with a particular focus on the word *you*, which will reinforce that your presentation is all about the client.
3. Pay attention to opportunities to use numbers to grab the audience's attention and make your presentation concrete and credible.

7

Making It Compelling

Myth: People buy benefits.
Truth: People buy *compelling* benefits.

Most sales professionals have had some exposure to sales training—and even those who haven't are probably familiar with the fundamental concept of features and benefits. I have found that, when asked, people understand that a *feature* is a fact about or characteristic of a product, and a *benefit* is an advantage or attribute of a product. Speaker and sales training expert Eric Baron summarizes this succinctly: A feature answers the question, "What?" A benefit answers the question, "So what?" Most of us know that customers buy benefits, not features. It is therefore important in a sales presentation to highlight the benefits.

Seems simple, right? It should be. But although this is an easy concept to grasp intellectually, it can be surprisingly difficult to implement during the actual sales presentation.

This has a lot to do with our perspective. As salespeople, we live in a sea of features. And since these features' benefits are so clear to us, we take for granted that they are clear to everyone else. We assume that clients will connect the feature dots to the benefits dots like we do. But the truth is that we need to connect these dots for them.

71

I cannot tell you how often I ask (or one of our other coaches asks) the question when coaching deals: "So what?", or "Who cares?" In other words—why should this matter to the client? Sometimes team members will answer the question in a way that prompts us to ask these very same questions again. By the end of the coaching, everyone is jumping in as if they are listening with a different pair of ears—the client's. These ears are critically important when determining how to express yourself in a sales presentation. You need to craft your message with the clients' ears in mind, knowing that they will be listening for you to answer the question, "What can you do for me?"

All Benefits Are Not Created Equal

We conducted a workshop a few years back designed to help a sales force sell a guaranteed income product to participants in a retirement plan. I divided the group into two: I had half list the product's features and the other half list the benefits. Both groups had the words "guaranteed income" on their list. When I asked the entire group on which list this phrase belonged, they believed it belonged on both. They argued that while it is a feature of this product—in that it is structured to provide guaranteed income—it could also be considered a benefit as it *guarantees* income. While I understood the group's rationale in labeling it as a benefit, it is not what I would call a *compelling* benefit.

Compelling benefits are both relevant to the particular client needs being addressed and speak to the core of their interests in such a way that it moves them to buy, because it arouses their emotions. While these salespeople might argue that guaranteed income is a benefit, it is likely to be much more compelling to participants if you connect it with their core needs. And these are the needs that are most alive at three o'clock in the morning.

"May I try on a pair of the <u>client's</u> shoes please?"

Three-O'clock-in-the-Morning Language

Almost everyone has had the experience of waking up in the middle of the night and worrying about something. If you are like most people over the age of 40, this is an all too familiar experience. My personal time is 3:00 a.m.

Imagine participants in a retirement plan who lost much of their savings in 2008 and had to postpone their retirement. Do you think their first thought when they wake up in the middle of the night is, "Gosh, I wish I could have guaranteed income when I retire"? I don't think so. They are more likely thinking, "What am I going to do if I outlive my savings?" or, "At this rate, I will never be able to retire!" or, "I don't want to be a burden on my children." These thoughts are *real*, as they have emotion tied to them. (In fact, if emotion were not tied to them, we would all be getting a better night's sleep!)

For a benefit to be really compelling, it needs to be:

- *Particularly important* to this specific client (address his or her specific problem, opportunity, or need)
- Framed in a way that will *resonate on an emotional level*

Following is a list of features and their corresponding benefits. While the benefit is in fact a benefit in a traditional sense, it is not necessarily a *compelling* benefit. The far right column gives an example of how a benefit could be framed to be more compelling to a client. Of course, in order for any benefit to be truly compelling, it needs to speak to that specific client's situation and tune into his or her three-o'clock-in-the-morning language. And the best way to know that is to do your homework long before the final presentation.

Feature	Benefit	Compelling Benefit
Detailed workflows	Ensure a seamless transition	So you won't be interrupted by frustrated employees
Call center with response times less than one minute	Eliminates long wait times	So no one gets irritated pushing buttons and waiting to speak with a human being
A dashboard that tracks your pipeline	So you know where every deal is in the sales cycle	So there are no surprises and you can feel confident that your projections will be on target
An account manager with 15 years experience in your industry	A person who is familiar with all the nuances	So you can be confident that person will hit the ground running and that recommendations will be on target and relevant
Automatic enrollment in the retirement plan	More people will be on the right path for retirement	So you can rest assured you are doing everything that you can to help people save for their retirement

As simple as the concept of features and benefits are, you have to be disciplined to ensure that you are actually connecting the features of your product, service, or capability with the benefits so that clients will be excited about your offer and see how it can ultimately help them get a better night's sleep!

CHALLENGE

When rehearsing for your next sales presentation, ask everyone who's listening to pay close attention to whether the messages are answering the questions: "So what?" or "Why should the client care?" Pay attention to the language that people are using. Challenge everyone to use language that the client might be using when thinking about their problems (especially at three o'clock in the morning).

What We Are *Really* Selling

Our tendency is usually to think about features and benefits in terms of the products and services we offer a client. We have talked a lot about the sales presentation as an *experience* at this point. This notion of experience also extends to what we are selling and what clients are buying.

Back in the late 1990s, my husband and I were in the market for a new SUV that would accommodate all the stuff that comes with a young family (car seats, diaper bags, strollers, babysitter, etc.). The Land Rover seemed to be the popular SUV of the day, so we decided to go to the closest dealer to check one out. As we pulled up to the dealership, we parked next to a driving course designed to look like a mountain, on which a Land Rover was poised halfway up. This driving course did not have even the slightest resemblance to the suburban Fairfield County roads that we would follow to get our family and our stuff to the grocery store, nursery school, and back home again. In fact, I don't think any terrain within 300 miles of us looked anything like this brick-red mountainous sculpture sitting in the parking lot of this dealership.

Well, the driving course was only the beginning of the picture that this dealership was strategically painting—and somewhere during the buying cycle, we fell hook, line, and sinker for the "adventure" that Land Rover was selling. We ended up with a new hunter-green Land Rover (new car smell and all). When we went to pick it up, we were congratulated on deciding to take the adventure and given all sorts of adventure paraphernalia, including a compass, a keychain, and a tin of popcorn with adventure images (perhaps for sustenance?). About a month into our so-called adventure, we received an impressive blank journal (that must have cost about $25 to produce) so that we could log our "journey." Adventure-oriented mailing pieces continued to show up in our mailbox every few months for the three or four years that we owned the car.

Looking back at this now, it is very clear to me that the people at Land Rover were masters at selling an *experience*. At the time, we had also looked at the Toyota Land Cruiser. The Toyota salespeople gave us the complete rundown on the engine size, safety, features (and benefits!) of the easy-to-maneuver third seat. However, they were merely attempting to sell an SUV. Land Rover was selling an *experience*, the promise of an adventure, to young parents who were just a little concerned (as many new parents are) that the adventures of parenthood would be limited to tending scraped knees and changing dirty diapers.

When preparing for a sales presentation, we not only need to pay close attention to the sales experience that we are creating, we also need to think about the *experience* associated with what we are selling. Services, by nature, are experiences. Helping clients to understand what their experience will be like when they work with you and use your products and services can be the most effective way to access the buying committee's emotions—and make your offer memorable.

I know, for example, that my colleagues and I are not just selling training workshops and coaching sessions. We are selling the *experience* that our clients will have working with us, as well as the *experience* that *their* salespeople will have when participating in one of our workshops or coaching sessions. In fact, one of the hallmarks of what we do is to help people *experience* the success of a new behavior. That way, we know that they will own the behavior forever.

The Art of Storytelling

In the first section of the book, I asked you to think about the presentation as a story with a beginning, a middle, and an end. I suggested that you create a storyboard for your presentation and identify the stories within the story that could bring it to life. Everyone tells stories; it is a natural part of how humans communicate. In fact, it's often something we do without even knowing we are doing so; yet some of us are better storytellers than others. This chapter provides some guidelines on how to tell a story so that it accomplishes what you want it to.

If you have children—or brothers and sisters—you will probably agree that no one provides direct feedback quite like siblings do. My teenage boys are no exception. In our house, one boy is quick to point out to the other that his story is boring by injecting the line, ". . . and then you found five dollars." In other words, "Your story is boring and pointless and needs an ending that is worth at least five dollars."

We need to be careful that our stories during the sales presentation are not boring or pointless. We must ensure that any story we tell supports the point that we are trying to make—and that the point is crystal clear to the client. While we often assume that clients will "just get it," we need to *help them* get it, in most cases.

I often suggest that people frame their stories by revealing the point of the story *before* the actual story and then repeating the point again afterward. This is the same principal as, "Tell them what you are going to tell them; tell them; and then tell them what you told them." Following is an example of how I might frame a story that

I sometimes tell when I am presenting to a client on the power of coaching.

> *I want to tell you a story that illustrates why follow-up coaching is so important after sales training to ensure that you get the impact you expect.*
>
> When completing a workshop many years ago, the sales manager asked me to come back the following week to coach on a finals presentation for a big and important deal. Most of the people on the deal team had participated in the program and were very complimentary of it. As a consequence, all were excited to have a coach help them through the deal. As I entered the large conference room, already abuzz with team members tossing papers back and forth, I was handed the presentation. The first thing I noticed was that the presentation began with *their company*—not the client's, which of course was contradictory to what we had discussed and practiced in the workshop. When I asked them why, Brian— the salesperson leading the team—said, "Well we have always done it this way, and this deal is so important, we can't afford to take any chances." I reminded the group of the rationale behind the approach I had taught and held their hand as they struggled with their resistance to try something new. Something occurred to me in that moment: Even though people may intellectually buy into a new behavior in a classroom situation, they will revert to their standard—and comfortable—behavior when the stakes are high. Coaching can help bridge what they learn in the classroom to real client situations, and we know once we get people to experience the success of a new behavior, they will own it forever. That is where you get the highest return on your investment.
>
> *I tell you this story because it really drives home the importance of follow-up coaching as part of your training plan.*

You will notice that I told them the point of the story *before* I actually told them the story, and then I told them what I wanted them to take away from the story after I told it. It is not enough to tell a great story; you also need to make sure the audience understands precisely *why* you are telling it.

Telling effective stories in a sales presentation usually takes some planning and practice. But once we have honed a story, it becomes a part of our tool kit—something that we can pull out at the appropriate time. Many books and workshops go into great depth on the art of storytelling. For the purposes of this book, I have outlined a simple set of guidelines for you to think about as you craft your stories:

1. Make sure your message for the story is clear.
   a. *Why* do you want to tell this story?
   b. What do you hope to *accomplish*?
   c. *What point* do you want to get across?
   d. *What emotion* (e.g., excitement, fear, confidence, trust) do you want to spur?
2. Use *names, characters, places*—anything you can to make it as real as possible for the audience. Use your words to draw pictures as well. ("There were wall-to-wall flip charts, even on the windows!")
3. Use words and phrases that convey *passion and emotion*. ("It was so frustrating for the client." "We were all so excited when we found what we were looking for—we could have popped the champagne right there!")

The following is one of my favorite stories, one that I often tell in workshops to bring to life the power of stories in a sales presentation. I was fortunate enough to work with the main character in this story many times—an incredibly talented and graceful woman who sadly passed away about a year after this took place. The story happened several years ago, when I was contracted to coach a very important deal for a long-time client. The company had been selected as a finalist for a large shipping company's retirement plan. A significant amount of time and energy had gone into taking the deal this far—and the stakes were high. The team was meeting for a final rehearsal the day before the sales presentation. As you might imagine, there was a constant buzz of energy as we refined messaging, confirmed timing, and practiced transitions. In typical war-room style, you could barely see the tabletop; it was covered with binders, laptops, notepads, and BlackBerrys.

We took a short break for lunch, and as we moved papers aside to make room to eat, one of the team members—told me and a few of the other team members something: "This deal has a great deal of personal significance to me." She went on to explain that this client was largely responsible for getting her to where she was today. Her father had been a longtime driver for the company, and his employment had allowed her and her brother to be the first ones in their family to get college degrees. She told us that her dad had actually been inducted into a coveted society that the client had established to recognize those who have achieved 25 years or more of accident-free driving. Several more members of the team had joined us by now, and we all proclaimed (almost in unison), "You have *got* to tell that story!" She immediately agreed. After the big day, we had a call to debrief the presentation. As the team recounted the meeting, they told me with great enthusiasm that the tone of the whole presentation changed after the story was told. One of the team members described the feeling in that room: "It was as though we suddenly went from being on opposite sides of the table to being on the same side." While we had all been impressed by her father's accomplishments, we did not know just how big an honor the induction was—and how admired it is within the shipping company.

We do not always have such strong opportunities to connect with clients at this level, but I can tell you with confidence that I have yet to find a situation where we cannot make an authentic connection through a story if we *really think about it.*

I tell you this to demonstrate how powerful storytelling can be. Personal anecdotes like these help to foster those critical personal and emotional connections between the sales team and the client team.

Of course, as the best stories do, this one has a happy ending. They won the deal.

CHALLENGE

1. Identify three to five key points that you typically need to make in your sales presentations.
2. Think about a personal experience that will support each point.
3. Write out how you would like to tell the story. Remember to start and end with the point of the story.
4. Edit it.
5. Practice it.
6. Refine it.
7. Tell it.

Say It with Passion—Enthusiasm Sells

"Your enthusiasm is contagious!" We have all heard this at one time or another. It seems that some people just tend to be enthusiastic by nature. They love, love, *love* the movie; they couldn't put the book down; they went on the *best* vacation ever! Most of the time, we become excited along with them. When you ask such people how they are, you don't get the standard, "Fine, thanks. How are you?" You get a robust response like, "I'm fabulous!" or "Fantastic!" If they respond in kind (". . . and how are you?"), most people find it hard to give the standard, "Fine, thanks." Their energy has been impacted, and they are therefore more likely to respond just (or almost) as enthusiastically.

The English word *enthusiasm* comes from the Greek *enthusiasmos*, which means "to inspire." Inspiration is at the heart of sales.

To become enthusiastic, you must act enthusiastically—because this is where thought and emotion connect. You cannot be enthusiastic about something without thinking and feeling positive about it.

Consider it a gift if you are the kind of person who shares your enthusiasm easily (probably not at the poker table, but most definitely in the sales presentation). Use it. Do not feel that you have to squelch it for the boardroom setting. It is refreshing, and it is powerful.

Even if enthusiasm runs strong in your DNA, you cannot *fake* it—because it comes from your deepest core. You have to really love your product, your organization, and your job. You don't have to love *every* aspect of them, but you need to feel good enough about them to show how proud and excited you are when bringing them to prospects and clients. If you cannot find something to love about each of these three, you should probably consider moving someplace where you can—because without enthusiasm, you are playing a game with one hand tied behind your back.

There will occasionally be one team member who cannot get past the fact that behind the scenes the organization is not as fine-tuned as he or she thinks it should be. Sometimes whole organizations succumb to an inferiority complex because they know deep down inside that they are not perfect. Beware: Negativism is just as contagious as enthusiasm.

Believe me, after 16 years of consulting and 11 years before that working for a large financial institution, I have seen some dirty laundry. In fact, it seems to be the very same laundry from one organization to the next. Don't get hung up on the laundry! Remember, everyone has it, and in most cases they do just fine with it. It is important when you go to the sales presentation that you leave that dirty laundry in the closet where it belongs. Tidy up what you can, and don't for a minute think that your competitors' closets are all perfectly folded, fresh, and white. This is just not how the world works.

Of course, while you cannot fake enthusiasm, you can always choose to be more enthusiastic—and, as a result, you will have more fun. This means different things to different personality types. If you are a stoic John Wayne–type, you do not need to assume Richard Simmons's bubbly, over-the-top personality. You just want to be you—you on your best day, that is. Regardless of your natural inclination for enthusiasm, always be aware of the energy that you are putting out—whatever it is will likely come back to you.

Say It with Conviction

Phrases such as "we think" and "we believe" are weaker than "we know." "We hope" is weaker than "we expect."

I have come across a few people in my career who are pros at saying things in a way that does not invite any question, because what they say sounds like fact. You just *believe* them. I am not suggesting that you state things as fact when they are not; however, you should always speak with authority and confidence on things that you know. Sometimes we forget that we are the experts and know significantly more than our clients do about our subject. Clients want to have confidence in our expertise. We risk losing deals if we fail to convey this confidence.

I always cringe when I hear someone say, "If we are fortunate enough to work with you, we will . . ." We want the client to feel fortunate to work with *us*, not in a presumptuous or conceited way, but in a way that communicates that we provide value to our clients. I would prefer to hear simply, "When working with you, we will . . ." or "As your relationship manager, my first step will be . . ." or "As we move though the transition process, the key factors are . . .". Go ahead, believe that you will get the business—you deserve it!

Here is a passage from Harvey Mackay's book, *The Mackay MBA of Selling in the Real World*, which I think sums up this chapter up nicely:

> If you're in sales, you can have a great product, a tremendous territory and a fabulous marketing campaign, but if you don't have passion, it's hard to make a sale. When you have

passion, you speak with conviction, act with authority, and present with zeal. When you are excited and passionate about a product—or anything for that matter—people notice. They want in on the action. They want to know what can be so good.

If You Remember Only Three Things:

1. When you are explaining the benefit of a product, service, or experience, tune into your clients' three-o'clock-in-the-morning language (i.e., the language they are likely to use when they wake up in the middle of the night).
2. Realize that you are not just selling products and services, you are also selling the experience that your clients will have working with you.
3. Stories are the most powerful tool in the toolbox. Make sure their point is crystal clear by framing them. Bring passion and enthusiasm to the table, and always say what you want to say with conviction.

Interview with Denise Byrd Gangi

Denise sits on both sides of the sales table. As vice president of strategy and business development at Broadridge, a leading provider of investor communications and technology-driven solutions, Denise is often on both the selling and the buying side. In her previous role at IBM Global Services, she was responsible for outsourcing contracts, financial structuring, and negotiation, where she was frequently a member of a sales team.

On the importance of defining the problem . . .

My advice to a sales team is to focus on the pain point or the problem that you are trying to solve instead of trying to fit what you have into a solution. Don't try to sell us a cookie-cutter solution for a complex problem. Problems are typically multifaceted and may require several solutions. There are no magic bullets, so don't pretend that there are and that you can do it all. Know your strength and sweet spot, and be clear on what you can and can't solve.

On the use of anecdotes as proof points . . .

Use anecdotes to illustrate how you have solved a similar problem for a similar client. It brings what you are saying to life and demonstrates that you know how to do what you say you do. Showing and telling is especially helpful. I like to see sample deliverables; it provides value in that very moment.

Her top three pieces of advice:

1. It is always hard to know who the decision makers really are; in fact, they may not even be in the room when you are presenting. This is why you have to tell a story that can easily be retold—and why you want to leave behind materials that will help them to replicate the key points.
2. There is value in doing the basic things right. Arrive early. You may get an opportunity to chat with the client and connect on an individual level before the presentation.
3. Don't come to me with three hours of material when you have only one hour in which to present. We just went through an RFP process where all three presenters went over the one and half hours we gave them.

8 Anticipating and Answering Questions

The questions that clients ask, the manner in which salespeople address them, and the answers that they provide can make or break a deal. The question-and-answer component of the sales presentation is the most difficult for which to prepare, because it forces us to deal with the unknown. We can never be certain what clients will ask, why they ask it, and whether our answer will satisfy them.

Let's first take a look at what motivates clients to ask questions in a sales presentation:

- To *engage in the discussion* (they want to dialogue with you and participate in the meeting)
- To *elicit or clarify information* (they want to better understand you and your offer)
- To *test your knowledge* or to see how you will respond to pressure (they want to see whether you are credible and what you will be like to work with)
- To *compare you to the competition* (they are looking for how your answer will be different)
- To *look and feel smart* (in front of you, their colleagues, or both)
- *They feel they should* ask questions (i.e., it is expected of them, by either you or their colleagues, managers, and/or employees)

There are two components we should consider when we answer a question: *what* we say (the content) and *how* we say it (the skill). Of the two, the *what* tends to be the easiest to address. While there are typically some gnarly questions—and occasionally one or two that stop us in our tracks—we can usually plan for these in advance and figure out the best responses. On the other hand, *how* you answer can be very tricky—because it requires skill, quick thinking, and often a little help from your friends.

Anticipating questions that a buying committee is likely to ask, and then strategizing the answers, is a critical component of preparing for a sales presentation. The sales team *must* take time to put themselves in the client's shoes once again—this time, specifically by imagining the possible questions that may arise and identifying which team member is best equipped to answer each one. Role-playing those potentially difficult questions, and how you will answer them, is always is a good investment of your sales team's time. And when I say *role-play*, I mean it literally. One person pretends that he or she is the client, and the other person answers *in character*. This is important, as the team will be able to listen to the answer *as the client would* and then provide specific feedback to the person answering. Otherwise, only the content will be shared, and the team will not be able to get a sense of how this answer will make the client feel.

Common Mistakes

Here are the most common mistakes we see people make when answering questions in a sales presentation:

- *Answering the question without understanding what the client is asking.* We often do not fully listen to a question, because we are two steps ahead; we are expecting a certain question, so we hear it the way we are expecting to hear it. This causes us to miss what the client is really asking, which isn't good for anyone.

- *Assuming that we know why the client is asking the question.* Clients ask questions for all kinds of reasons (some, but not all, of which were listed previously). We often make assumptions based on what we have heard from clients previously, or from our own biases and concerns. This is probably the most common mistake we see, which is why much of this chapter is devoted to addressing this challenge.

- *Overanswering the question by providing too much information.* Sometimes this comes from an effort to be as responsive as possible; sometimes it is driven by insecurity because we don't think the clients will like our answer; and sometimes it is driven out of pure enthusiasm—we love to talk about our stuff! Regardless of the motivation, it is always better to be as brief as possible, and then check with clients to see whether more information is needed.

- *Failing to truly answer the question.* Often, we do this because we don't think the clients will like our answer, other times because we don't have an answer, and sometimes we just get lost in our own thought process.

- *Not checking to see whether we've answered the question to the clients' satisfaction, and how they feel about the answer.* In this case, we assume that we have answered the right question, given them enough information, and that they are satisfied with the answer—when in fact they may not be.

PET PEEVE

How many times have you been in a meeting where someone has asked a question to which there is an adequate response, yet another person jumps in to answer it again, adding no additional value? If we are really on a roll, it might even be answered again by a third person!

One of the most important things you can do to avoid these mistakes is to be conscious of them. Recognize that they are common, be on the lookout for them, and plan for ways to avoid them.

It is important that the team members support each other as they field these questions during presentations. For example, if you feel that the question is not clear, you might say to a fellow presenter something like this: "Max, before we answer that question, I would love to ask George [the client] for a little more context. This way, we can be certain that we're giving him the information that he is looking for."

If a team member has answered a question and has forgotten to check back, jump in with, "George, did that answer your question?" Or, if you want to get a feeling for the client's level of satisfaction, say, "George, does that make sense?" or perhaps, "Did that answer meet your expectations?"

Types of Questions

Two types of questions most commonly surface during sales presentations:

1. Questions that are asked to *elicit information*
2. Questions that are asked to *mask objections*

It is not always easy to determine which is which, and it can be dangerous to assume that we know the difference. When a client asks a close-ended question, always answer the question first. Let's say the client asks, "Do you have any offices overseas?"

Well, you either do or you don't, so just answer it. The answer is clear in this case: "No, Charlie, we do not."

But then you should follow up to find out whether there's a hidden meaning behind the question by saying, "Why do you ask?"

If the salesperson just jumps in immediately with "Why do you ask?" *without* first answering the question, it may sound as though he or she is avoiding the question. This is why, when you receive a yes-or-no, fact-based question, you should always answer it first—then find out why the client is asking.

Charlie might have a simple answer: "I was in Singapore last week, and saw an office building with the same name as yours; I was just curious."

This answer requires a minimal response, "No, that wasn't us, although I do love Singapore!"

However, what if Charlie answers this way: "Well, our last provider was so focused on its global development that it seemed to have forgotten the clients that were right in its own backyard!"

Such an answer provides an opportunity to reinforce your commitment to service: "We know how important service is to you, and I can assure you that will not be the case here. We pride ourselves in our responsiveness to our clients. That is one of the reasons why we have the regional organizational structure we do."

Suppose Charlie answers with something like this: "While there is nothing at play at the moment, we are thinking of expanding overseas and need a partner who can service us there."

In this case, the sales team would want to elicit more information so that they can understand what the client's real need is. After doing this, the presenter may say something like this: "It sounds to me as though you need a provider who is going to be able to support your growth overseas, that you want to be certain the infrastructure is there to provide the highest levels of service. Is that right? While we do not have brick-and-mortar offices in Singapore, we have the infrastructure. In fact, we have many clients with offices in Asia and have been able to provide them with service just as excellent overseas as it is domestically."

Each of these answers from the client requires a different response from the salesperson. Many salespeople assume that they know *why* the client is asking the question and respond to that assumption. In this case, a salesperson might assume that Charlie is asking because he needs you to have an office in Singapore. But if the salesperson responding to the question does not first find out why the client is asking, that salesperson probably would have gone on the defensive—and given a long explanation that could have been off-putting to the client.

In Chapter 7, I used an example about a guaranteed retirement income product. When we were training this sales force on how to introduce it to participants within a retirement plan, some team members were concerned that the plan participants would associate the product with traditional annuities, which had some bad press for being inflexible and expensive. Here's one of the questions they were concerned about fielding: "Is this an annuity?" Well, technically, it is. However, it's structured in a way that eliminates the negative aspects of a traditional annuity.

We began to role-play a few different scenarios and found that, time and again, the salesperson was asked by the individual who was role-playing the plan participant, "Is this an annuity?" The salesperson would then respond with a long-winded, detailed explanation that it was "kind of an annuity, but not *really* an annuity." In other words, the salesperson did not answer the question at all. Our advice to the group was to first answer the question. In this case the answer is, "Yes, this product is an annuity." We then advised the salesperson to ask, "What is your experience with annuities?" If the role-playing "client" answered by saying something either positive or neutral (e.g., "I don't know much about them," or, "I heard that I should consider an annuity"), the salesperson should just move on.

However, if the answer was, "Well, I want to stay away from those—I have heard that they are very inflexible," then the salesperson could take the opportunity to explain that while, technically, it *is* an annuity, it has been designed so that flexibility is built right in.

If the salesperson automatically jumps in with the second response in this scenario, this would prompt the client to become concerned about flexibility—something that had never crossed the client's mind until the *salesperson* brought it up. The salesperson now has to overcome an objection that was never an objection in the first place—whew!

This is one of those cases where our brains are too fast for our own good. We automatically connect our previous conversation with the conversation we are having at that moment. We assume we know what's going on in the mind of the person with whom we are speaking when there's no way we could. We hear so much of the same that we assume everyone and every situation are the same. But we have to remember to slow down, ask questions, and really listen with the intent to understand and to learn from our clients during the sales process.

CHALLENGE

In preparation for your next sales presentation:

- List all the potential questions—using the wording in which the client might ask them.
- Assign the person best qualified to answer that question to respond for the team.
- Have everyone on the team review their questions and identify those that might need further clarification.
- Role-play questions in character, and provide feedback to each other.

Guidelines for Answering Questions

Following are some general guidelines you can apply when fielding questions in a sales presentation. Of course, how and when you use them will of depend on each situation.

- *Listen very carefully* to the question the client is asking. If the question is not clear to you, ask for clarification.
- *Do not assume that you know why* clients are asking the question. Try to elicit their thinking or reasoning by asking a follow-up question.

If it is a yes-or-no question or a fact—*answer first with yes, no, or by stating the fact.* Then elicit more information to help you determine why they are asking, and go from there.

If it is an *open-ended question*, tell them that you would be happy to answer it—but that *you would like them to expand on it* to make sure you are addressing what is important to them.

- *Keep your answers short* and to the point.
- After you answer, *check back with the clients* to make sure you answered their question.
- *Elicit their reaction* to your answers. While you may be hesitant to do this for fear of a negative reaction, it's better to get it on the table so that you have an opportunity to resolve their objection.

Helpful Phrases

Following are some phrases that you might consider adding to your repertoire if you do not already use them. They will serve you well when answering clients' questions in the heat of the moment.

To *confirm you understand* the question:
- "Let me see if I understand your question." Then restate the question or ask for further clarification.

To *gain insight into why* they are asking the question:
- "I am happy to answer that question. Can you share a little more about your perspective so that I can be sure to address what you need me to?"

To *be certain that you answered the question*:
- "Did I answer your question?" This is fairly straightforward!

To *elicit information* about how your answer has been received:
- "Does that make sense?"
- "Can you share a little bit about your thinking?"
- "Is that what you were expecting?"

Regardless of the situation, it is important that you answer clients' questions with confidence and conviction. They want to be sure that you know your stuff, are responsive, and can get the job done. Asking questions, listening to your answers, and observing how you answer them will give the buying committee a snapshot of your thinking processes and let them know what you will be like to work with.

When You Don't Know the Answer . . .

Even the most prepared and knowledgeable salespeople will find themselves in situations where they do not have the answer. And we have all probably figured out by now that if we don't have the answer, we certainly shouldn't make it up. Assuming that the question the client has asked is *not* something that you should know cold, there is no need to apologize. Even when a client has asked an outlandish or very technical question, I often hear salespeople start their reply with an apology: "I am sorry, Charlie, but I don't know the answer to that." I much prefer to hear them answer it simply: "That is a great question, Charlie. I don't have the answer for you right now, but I will make sure I have it first thing in the morning. Can I get back to you on that tomorrow?" This also gives you a wonderful opportunity for follow-up.

I am sometimes asked what to do if a teammate provides a wrong answer, and my response is, "It depends." If the information is critical to the client's decision making, then I think you need to jump in and correct the information while doing your best to protect your teammate's credibility. "Marcia, you are always two steps ahead of the game. While that capability will be available the first of next year, I do not believe it is available now—but we will, of course, confirm that."

However, if the wrong answer is a minor infraction and not very substantive, you can let it go and correct it, as necessary, during your follow-up.

If You Remember Only Three Things:

1. Plan how you will answer anticipated questions, and role-play the difficult ones, in character.
2. Before answering questions, make sure you understand what the clients are asking and why they are asking it.
3. Always check back with clients to make sure that you answered their question—and elicit their reaction to your answer whenever possible.

9

Behaving as a Team: Team Dynamics

In earlier chapters, I talked about the real reason everyone comes together for final presentations: so that the client can experience and assess what it is like to work with you compared to your competitors. Therefore, the explicit and implicit messages that you send about how you work with others are critical.

I remember attending a training session many years ago with a very highly regarded consulting firm that helped individuals and organizations work better with one another. The company's approach was grounded in linguistics, and the goal was to help people to think and perform outside of their traditional realm of possibilities. I had previously attended several other programs put on by this firm, and I always came away thinking slightly differently than when had I arrived—a mark of a good program.

This particular session was being team-facilitated by two women, and it became very apparent during the first hour that there was conflict between the two. Even though they were polite and professional to one another, I could sense an air of competitiveness. It wasn't a particular comment that either of them made or a look that one gave the other, but something was just amiss—like a disagreeable odor in the room. And it was distracting. Of course, it was also disconcerting that they were supposed to be practicing what they were preaching.

You can be absolutely certain that buying committees can easily pick up on a team's chemistry—and that it *will* impact their buying decision. Therefore, it is crucial to keep team dynamics in mind when preparing for a presentation. Creating positive chemistry can be particularly challenging in organizations in which the selling teams change frequently and members have developed little or no relationship with one another before sales presentations.

While you clearly cannot manufacture chemistry, being conscious of its importance—and providing opportunities for the team to interact with each other—can accelerate its development. This is why I like to invest 5 or 10 minutes at the beginning of strategy sessions and rehearsals to do a warm-up exercise. It can be as simple as asking people to share something that they are passionate about outside of work. I encourage them to bring that passion to the sales presentation when I use this warm-up. Here are some other warm-up ideas:

- What was the highlight of your summer?
- What is your favorite holiday tradition (if it's near a holiday)?
- What is your best childhood summer memory (as summer approaches)?
- What is your dream vacation?
- Share your memory of your very first presentation. (This one is particularly helpful when there are inexperienced and potentially nervous presenters on the team. They are likely to take comfort in knowing that others can relate to their experience at one time or another.)

I also suggest that the sales team get together for dinner or a little downtime the night before a big presentation. This allows them to enjoy each other's company outside of the business setting. A shared meal and a laugh can go a long way in building a team's rapport.

In addition to encouraging bonding, salespeople can do some very tactical things during presentations to help support each other and to ensure that they are behaving as a team. While your team members have all (we hope!) heard each other practice several times before the big day, everyone should be as engaged during the presentation as if they were hearing each other for the very first time.

I am in front of groups often—sometimes in small workshop situations, sometimes in large auditoriums. But no matter how small or large the group is, I can usually find at least one or two people in the audience who feel like my champions. They smile from the start. They appear to be totally engaged. They nod frequently and laugh at my jokes. When I ask the group a question, they are the first to respond. I appreciate these people, and I try to *be* one of these people myself when I am an audience member.

Be this person for your teammates. Give them all of your attention and positive energy. Nod or smile to let them know that you think they are doing a good job. This does two very important things: First, it boosts their confidence; second, it signals to the client that you are in fact a team of supportive people who like to work together.

Other behaviors signal to the client that you operate as a cohesive team and enjoy working together:

- Using each other's names
- Demonstrating engagement through body language (nodding, leaning forward, eye contact, tracking with the materials)
- Smiling
- Laughing at one another's jokes (even when you have heard them before!)
- Referencing a team member's earlier comment ("As John said . . .")
- Sensitively stepping in if a team member needs help answering a question or managing equipment or materials.

Tradition: Hand over the floor to teammates by reminding the client of their name, title, and what they will talk about.

New tradition: Hand over the floor to teammates with fanfare! Create enthusiasm and excitement for the next person your audience is going to hear.

One of the most powerful opportunities to sell the team happens when one team member transitions to another. A team member will typically transition to another team member by saying something like, "Thank you. I will now hand over the floor to Kathleen, who will talk to you about implementation."

This kind of transition represents an enormous missed opportunity to build a team member's credibility and create anticipation and excitement for the next speaker. Contrast the previous introduction with the following: "I am pleased to be able to hand over the floor to Kathleen, who will be responsible for ensuring a smooth and seamless transition from your current provider to us. No one I know has as keen attention to detail and as strong a commitment to exceeding client expectations as Kathleen. Though she won't tell you this, Kathleen has recently been awarded one of our organizations highest honors, which recognizes commitment to client service—this is why I know you will love working with her. Kathleen . . . [handing over the floor]?"

Team members can brag about their colleagues in a way that those colleagues would never be able to brag about themselves. In this example, a client is likely to be excited about Kathleen's attention to detail and her strong commitment to exceeding client expectations. What resonates even more is the acknowledgment that she received. Who would not be excited about Kathleen after hearing that? Colleagues can also help to highlight each other's personalities, as seen in the following example: "I am excited to be able transition the presentation over to Mike, whom I have had the opportunity to work with for a very long time. I can tell you with certainty that no one I know understands the intricacies of funding like Mike does. Not only that—but I have found him to be a very good loser on the golf course (but we won't go there right now)."

A genuine display of affection for your teammates will appeal to a buying committee. We all want to enjoy what we do and the people with whom we work. Communicating a work-hard/play-hard attitude can be powerfully attractive.

Transitions can also provide an opportunity to allow the buying committee to learn a little about the people on the team outside of the business setting. I remember one person who included in their transition, "Hannah is too modest to tell you this, but in addition to her outstanding actuary skills, she is a very accomplished concert pianist." Not only did this introduction showcase Hannah's human side, it signaled to the client that these people really like each other and are proud of each other's accomplishments—even personal ones.

I recently had two different people from the same organization introduce me before I began two separate workshops. One of them had asked me for my resume and, God bless him, had memorized just about all of it. He seemed to know it better than I did. He mentioned the first organization I had worked for and the positions I held there. He cited my current clients, the nature of my work, and my title. He had all of my information down cold. And although I appreciated the effort he put into it, I knew the introduction would get me just so far—and that I needed to work particularly hard to develop credibility with the audience.

The other person did not ask for my resume. In fairness, we had worked together on many occasions throughout the years (although I am quite certain that his knowledge of my resume was pretty much limited to his personal interaction with me). Here's how he began his introduction: "I am excited to introduce to you today someone who, by title, is a consultant, but in reality is a true partner—the kind of partner we aspire to be with our clients. She has had a very personal impact on my success and, in fact, most recently coached me and my team to winning a $500 million dollar deal." Wow! Me? *Really*? Even *I* was excited to hear me!

Now, as I climb down from my high horse, I must admit two things: First, shame on me for not preparing the first person to better introduce me (that was not his fault, but mine). The other is that the second person may have exaggerated a bit (though I am, of course, grateful).

I have found that people who have worked together many times think they know each other, but, oddly, may not know what they need in order to introduce each other in a compelling way. Because of this, I sometimes suggest that the members of the sales organizations with whom I work complete something I call a "brag sheet." This is simply a list of their personal and professional interests and accomplishments—and a tool that helps others know how to introduce them in the most flattering light.

BRAG SHEET

Awards, recognitions:
Industry experience:
What you like most about what you do:
Interests outside of work:
Information about your background that is likely to impress clients:

Just as we practice introductions in the rehearsal, we also plan out and practice every transition. I sometimes have people who are providing introductions work with the person they are introducing to come up with a powerful transition. Another benefit of this exercise is that everyone feels just a little bit better about themselves after hearing a colleague sing their praises!

Using Senior Executives in the Presentation

When done effectively, it can be extremely powerful to bring a senior executive to the sales presentation. A team with whom I recently worked said that they thought they had lost a previous deal largely because the competitor brought out the big guns and they had not. I am not sure whether that was the case or not; however, I do know that it can impress buying teams quite a bit when a senior-level executive comes to the table.

Early in my consulting career I was hired by Chase Manhattan Bank, my previous employer, to source a large training curriculum. When I think about senior executives being effective, I think back to a finals presentation in which Kevin Daley was in that role. He was the founder and president of Communispond, Inc., the top presentation consulting and training firm at the time. Kevin was well known in the industry, and his company was a finalist for the presentation skills component of the curriculum. The two women whom I had worked with through the RFP process presented, and Kevin sat on the sideline as an elder statesman. At the end of the presentation, he stood up for a few minutes and thanked the buying committee for inviting Communispond to present. He reiterated his firm's excitement at the prospect of working with Chase and his confidence in his team to get the job done.

While it can be incredibly effective to use a senior executive on a deal, it can also be riddled with problems. Let's address the reasons you might use a senior executive in the first place. There are four major ones:

1. To communicate to prospects or clients that they are *so important* that this high-powered—and highly paid individual—has taken time out of his or her busy schedule to attend the meeting.
2. To allow the buying committee to look in the eye the person with whom the buck stops.
3. To reinforce the firm's commitment to the business (if this is in question), assuring the buying committee that the firm is in it for the long run.
4. In a rebid situation, to assure the buying committee that a problem or issue has been corrected.

Whatever the objective, having a senior executive in tow can be stressful for a number of reasons. First of all, it is a challenging dynamic, because the salesperson is (or at least should be) running the show. This puts the salesperson in that awkward position of telling the senior executive what to say. This, of course, won't be a problem if you are dealing with a highly evolved individual and a supremely confident salesperson. But let's face it, this is not always the case. I have witnessed many presentations go awry in the absence of these characteristics. Either the salesperson did not give the senior executive enough direction, or the senior executive didn't listen—which usually ends up with the executive talking too long or taking over the show, leaving everyone else scrambling to adjust their sections of the presentation with the time that they have left.

Senior executives then repeat this performance, because salespeople tell them what they assume these higher-ups want to hear. When they ask the team how they did, executives are apt to hear, "You were great!" And really, who can blame the salespeople? Can you imagine telling a senior executive at your company that he or she *didn't* do a great job? However, this is what leads history to repeat itself—again and again.

A note to salespeople: Be as specific as you can when briefing senior leaders. Provide them with the information that they need to be successful. Be specific about the messages that you want them to convey and the time that they are allotted. When appropriate, provide specific talking points in advance of the presentation.

A note to senior leaders: Demand from your salespeople the information that you need to be successful. Be willing to practice and receive feedback. Follow the salesperson's parameters on time. Be sensitive to the fact that it will be difficult for people to give you candid feedback. Create an environment for them to do so; listen with the intent to learn; and thank them for being so honest.

Salespeople often ask me: At what point in the presentation should the senior leader speak? While this is largely dependent on the situation, I typically prefer to see senior executives speak at the end of the content of the presentation but before the close. Since their comments are typically about things like organizational commitment and industry perspective, it can act as an effective summary and final statement of commitment. If they do speak at the beginning, the remarks need to be client-centric. You want to avoid giving a big overview of your organization at the meeting's opening—and since the senior leader is usually delivering messages about his or her firm, this kind of statement is best left to the end.

In a scenario when it *does* make sense to have a senior executive speak at the opening, it should be at the beginning of the content. A salesperson or relationship manager should be opening and facilitating introductions. I always suggest that the senior leader be the last one to introduce him- or herself. This gives the executive an opportunity to briefly reinforce the team's credibility and the organization's commitment to the client.

In a recent coaching situation, one of the team members asked what I thought about senior executives taking notes in a sales presentation. She asked specifically whether I thought it was appropriate for senior executives to take notes at all, because she thought many of them, by not taking notes signaled through their behavior that they were "above it." She also thought that watching an executive pulling out a Sharpie and a legal pad and capturing everything that is said, as if he or she is taking dictation, may not be the best visual to reinforce that person's importance and level of seniority. I agreed with her assessment and shared with her an example of someone I thought struck an appropriate balance.

Our director of marketing, Kathleen Johnson, recently introduced me to her longtime friend and colleague, Michael Cole-Fontayn, who serves as chairman of Europe, the Middle East, and Africa and is global head of the ADR Group for the Bank of New York. We had lunch with him and two of his colleagues. A couple of times during our lunch conversation, he pulled an index card from his jacket to jot down a note on something that Kathleen or I had said. Whether he was aware of it or not, his actions were giving us a huge compliment by implying that he considered what we had said to be important. It also let us know that he was engaged in our conversation.

I thought Cole-Fontayn's approach was very appropriate for a man of his position. No one is too important to learn from someone else, nor brilliant enough to remember everything that is said (and if someone thinks so, he or she is probably not very likable).

No matter the seniority of the individuals on a sales team, it is important to consistently send the message to the buying committee that you are listening and care enough about what they have to say that you want to remember it. If buying committee members have a specific request of a senior executive or an issue that warrants his or her attention, they will take comfort in seeing that executive take a note or two.

The Team Makeup: Who and How Many?

I am often asked how many people should be on the presentation team. Of course, the answer is usually, "It depends." However, there *are* some general guidelines to consider:

- *Do not outnumber the buying committee.* One or two more people may be all right, but you do not want to overcrowd your audience.
- *Bring as few as possible to get the job done.* It's better to have too few than too many people on the team. The more people present, the harder the situation is to control—and the more difficult it is for the people in the room to form personal connections and engage in a dialogue. Having said this, you still need a large enough team for the client to feel you made an effort and that all bases are covered.
- *Do not bring anyone who is not necessary or anyone who will not have a speaking role.* Having someone sit there in silence can provide an awkward dynamic for both the client and the person who is not saying anything.

- *Do not bring people who are not fully prepared.* Before working with us, one of my clients had worked with a presentations coach who allowed the team members to use index cards to present (we are currently breaking them of this habit). It is never a good idea to use index cards or other notes; it sends a message to the client that the team members do not know enough about what they do and/or that they are not prepared.
- *Do not bring people who will not "play well" with the audience.* I recently coached a team that was presenting to a slick New York accounting firm. One member who had been assigned to the team was a quiet, sweet, young Midwestern girl. On meeting her, a few of the team members and I were concerned that she might not be a good match for the client's culture. Unfortunately, she could not be replaced just days before the finals. Although the deal was not lost, the buying committee requested that she be replaced. However, this young woman has done well with other clients who appreciated her friendly Midwestern demeanor.

Sales Leadership

It is the responsibility of sales managers to lead the team and ensure that team members are well versed on the client information. It's their job to coach team members in a way that helps them achieve their best possible performance. This, however, can be challenging, as in most cases, the team members do not report to the salesperson. It has been interesting for me to witness the differences in team presentations over the years. I've seen team members go above and beyond for one deal and those same team members do merely what is required of them on other deals. I believe that this divergence is largely due to leadership—or lack thereof. Some salespeople understand the important role of sales leadership to the success of deals, and it pays off for these people in spades. The best sales leaders:

- *Communicate.* One of the sales leader's most important roles is to ensure that team members have the information they need to be successful. It's also critical to continually provide updates on the deal. Updates are particularly important after the presentation, since this is the point at which people are invested and anxious for feedback.

- *Show appreciation to their team members.* Often, people need to rearrange both business and personal commitments to accommodate a deal schedule. I have found that most team members are more than happy to go the extra mile for an important sales presentation. However, they can become resentful if the salesperson doesn't appreciate and acknowledge their efforts—which diminishes their enthusiasm for the next deal. If a deal has required an extraordinary effort, provide extraordinary appreciation. I remember one salesperson sending a small box of Godiva chocolates to each team member with a note that read, "We've given it our best; all we can do now is wait and eat bonbons! Thanks for your extraordinary effort!"

- *Provide positive feedback to the team member and his or her manager.* If you feel particularly good about a team member's effort and performance, write a note of thanks—and copy his or her boss. This small investment of time will pay off handsomely: The team member will appreciate it, the boss will appreciate it, it will make you feel great, and everyone will line up to work with you again!

- *Coach team members on their presentation skills.* This can be difficult, as you want to provide constructive, developmental feedback without deflating their confidence. Following are some specific guidelines that will help you find this balance.

- *Motivate the team.* I spoke earlier about how enthusiasm sells, and the same notion holds true for your team. Let them know how excited you are about the client opportunity and how confident you are in them to bring the best of your organization to the client's doorstep.

Coaching the Team

Admittedly, not all salespeople are comfortable in this role. I recently conducted a needs analysis for a new client. One of the salespeople I spoke to complained about the presentation skill level of the team members that he brought out to finals presentations. I asked if there was any kind of training or coaching for them, and he told me that he did not think so. I asked whether he provided feedback to them on their presentation skills, and he said that he found it hard to do so, because they usually practiced just a day or two before the deal and he did not want to make them nervous or hinder their confidence. So, although this man wasn't happy about his team members' performance, he wasn't doing anything at all to help improve it.

Unfortunately, this scenario is not unusual—and it is further complicated when the team members who are going out on deals do not present very often. It is also challenging when the organization does not have a culture that values coaching, since coaching is essential to ensuring the team's highest possible performance.

Coaching Fundamentals

There are eight basic guidelines to successful coaching.

1. *Be selective about the behaviors and skills on which you focus your coaching.* Ask yourself the following questions:
   - Will the desired change have an impact on this person's performance in this deal?
   - Is this something that the person *can* reasonably change? Some things (e.g., personal attributes) are just not coachable. In other words, you cannot coach someone to be more intuitive, mature, or charismatic.
   - Is it realistic that this person will be able to change this behavior or skill between now and the presentation?
     When I coach people on their presentation skills, I first assess their skill level. I continually ask the question: How can I

bring them to their highest level of performance in the short time that we have to work while not overwhelming them? My goal is to always leave each person I coach with a high level of confidence. I always want to be conscious of that fine line between enough coaching to make a difference and too much coaching to create angst and insecurity.

Fortunately, some skills can be easily corrected.

2. *Highlight the successful skills of people you are coaching.* It is as important (if not more so) to point out the things that are working for them as to point out things they can improve. Recognizing positive skills or behaviors they exhibit will help them:
   - To repeat the behavior in the sales presentation
   - To be open to the corrective coaching
   - To increase their confidence

3. *Be specific.* As you observe someone, take notes that allow you to provide specific feedback. For example, instead of saying, "Your opening was really great," say, "I thought it was particularly powerful when you said in your opening that 'there are three things different in our approach'—and then you paused."

4. *Recognize that the people you are coaching are* not you. These individuals will bring their own personalities, skills, and knowledge to the table; your job is simply to help them be the best that they can be, while recognizing that they have to be themselves. Anything else will appear disingenuous.

5. *Focus on the goal.* The endgame is for each team member to foster confidence in the buying committee and to make personal, emotional, and professional connections. This should determine what you select to coach on. Don't get hung up on traditional best-practice presentation skills. For example, people are quick to self-criticize or point out each other's use of "ums." I don't mind these fillers if they do not distract from the presenter. In fact, President Obama uses "uh" quite a bit, and he has managed to do pretty well in spite of it. If, however, the

ums or other filler words distract from the message, then provide feedback at the appropriate time. Assuming the deal is imminent, consider waiting until after the presentation to mention anything, as these kinds of ingrained habits can be hard to break. It is unlikely that you will change the behavior in time for the presentation—and the risk of bringing this to the attention of presenters is that they can become so focused on breaking the habit that they will freeze up. Following are some guidelines to help you identify the easy fixes versus those behaviors or skills that tend to need to be coached over time— as well as those that you usually cannot change.

What to coach in the short term (easy fixes)	What to coach in the long term	Things that are typically not coachable
Specific messaging for the client	Habits such as fillers: um, ah, uh	Quality of voice Personality
Physical use of the body (standing, sitting, etc.)	Stance, how people use their bodies	Maturity Ability to think on feet
Incorporating stories, framing the story	Telling a powerful story	
Making eye contact	Better use of eye contact	
Smiling		
Questions that will likely be asked and how to answer them	Highlighting personality	
Clothing choices	Pitch, tone	
Handling nervousness	Effective use of the pause	
Pace and pausing		
Use of materials		

6. *While you cannot change attributes, you can help people see how they can leverage their most attractive characteristics.* If someone is funny, encourage him or her to use humor. If someone is sweet and approachable, encourage that person to tell stories from the

heart. If someone has a great smile, encourage that person to smile. Of course, the reverse also holds true. You do not want to coach someone to be funny if that is not within his or her comfort zone.

7. *Do not overwhelm someone with too much feedback.* Naming two or three positives and two or three ideas for improvement is plenty for one session.

8. *Ask for coaching yourself.* Listen to and apply the feedback you receive. Be appreciative of the feedback and the ideas offered to make you better. Model the behaviors that you would like to see in others.

TIPS ON MANAGING YOUR NERVES OR HELPING OTHERS MANAGE THEIRS

- *Breathe. Just breathe.* When we are nervous we tend to take shallow breaths, which results in nervous habits (and, even worse, feeling light-headed!). Be conscious about taking deep breaths through your nose and releasing them slowly through your mouth.

- *If possible, shake each person's hand before the presentation.* One-on-one physical contact can help to ease the feeling that you are presenting to strangers.

- *Know how your nerves affect you.* The extra adrenaline released when we are nervous impacts us physically. Some people may release this extra energy in their feet, resulting in foot tapping; others may release it in their hands by jiggling change; and others may release it in their legs, causing them to swivel their chairs. Being conscious of whatever tendencies you have will go a long way toward helping you manage your nervous habits.

- *Move.* If possible, try to burn off some of your excess energy before the presentation by jumping up and down in the restroom or, if that is not possible, by moving quickly (but not weirdly) as you set up the room.

Professional Coaching

I strongly recommend that sales organizations provide professional coaching for both their salespeople and other organization members who are called upon to participate in sales presentations. Coaching people on their presentation skills is one of my personal favorite kinds of coaching assignments because the results are immediate, and those being coached are usually very grateful for their enhanced skills. If you choose to hire professional coaches, make sure that they are well versed in sales and that they use video in their coaching. While most people are not particularly excited about the prospect of being videotaped, they almost always recognize its power in this process. Presentation coaching pays off for both the individual and the organization, and it can have a significant impact on close ratios.

Stand or Sit?

I am often asked whether I think people should stand or sit in a sales presentation. Again, it depends on the situation. If it is an informal setting where clients are expecting more of a dialogue than a presentation, I recommend sitting. It tends to be informal and supports a more interactive dialogue.

If, however, the presentation is at the end of a lengthy sales cycle that has culminated in a buying committee gathering to hear a select number of finalists, I recommend that the presenters stand. Having said this, I sometimes suggest that you mix it up a bit—with one or two members remaining seated for their part of the presentation. This is most fitting when this person's presentation is short, does not require any visual support, or the situation calls for more of a dialogue. I use this technique myself when facilitating workshops. If I want more of a discussion from the group, I will sit. If I need to command the attention of the room, I will stand.

When you stand and are using a screen to present, stand stage left. (If, by some crazy chance you were not a theater major, this is to the left of the screen as you are looking at it—that is, as an audience member will see it.) The reason for this is simple: People read from left to right, and the audience members' eyes will naturally come back to you (where you want it) after they have absorbed what is on the screen.

If you are ever faced with the option of using a podium, *avoid it at all costs*. Podiums act as a barrier between you and the audience. Fortunately, most of them are on wheels. You can easily reposition it so that it is to the side, perhaps doing the job of holding your laptop.

Power Poses

In 1989 a researcher by the name of Robert Zajonc published a significant study that linked facial changes associated with a smile to certain brain activities associated with happiness. This and subsequent studies prove that the mere act of smiling makes one happier. Imagine that! Just *faking* a smile has a positive impact on your feeling of happiness.

Along these same lines, Harvard Business School professor Amy Cuddy has studied the impact that body positions can have on our brain. She and collaborator Dana Carnie found that the mere act of a power pose will make you feel more powerful, just as the mere act of a low-power pose will make you feel less powerful.

In their study, Cuddy and Carnie contrast two common stances: the power position, which is big and open (think Popeye), and the low-power position, which is small and closed (think Olive Oyl).

In a highly engaging lecture captured on YouTube (www.youtube .com/watch?v=Y4386jSnFEU), Cuddy tells of a study in which participants' testosterone (commonly associated with power) and cortisol (commonly associated with stress) levels were tested when they entered her lab. After the test, participants were led into a room in which they were randomly asked to assume either a power position or a low-power position for two minutes. They were then asked a series of questions and provided an opportunity to participate in a small gambling activity designed to measure the participants' risk tolerance. This test was incorporated because people feel much more risk tolerant when they feel powerful. After this, participants' hormone levels were tested a second time.

The results of the study revealed that testosterone levels of those who assumed the high-power pose rose significantly, while their cortisol levels decreased significantly. Conversely, testosterone levels of those who had assumed the low-power pose decreased significantly, while their cortisol level increased significantly. What is amazing about this study is that the positions were assumed for only 2 minutes yet had a physiological impact for at least 17 minutes (when the second test was taken). The positions also affected behavior. High-power posers were significantly more likely to take the gamble that was offered than low-power posers.

What does all this have to do with the sales presentation? It is important that the participants act and feel powerful during a sales presentation. They may not need to take a superhero stance that suggests, "I will dominate this room," but they should stand in a way that conveys confidence in a "nobody can do this better" kind of way.

To facilitate an increase in testosterone before a presentation, Cuddy suggests that you find a private place where you can assume a power position in advance of the presentation. So, ladies—try striking your best Wonder Woman pose in the ladies room a few minutes before your next presentation. And gentlemen—abandon your Clark Kent for a few minutes in the men's room (too bad phone booths are a thing of the past).

The traditional superhero stance is definitely not appropriate in a sales presentation (i.e., it's more likely to elicit the response, "Who does he think he is?"). However, the following poses are both acceptable and powerful business positions:

- *Take as much space as possible when standing.* Use your hands and arms in a way that opens you up to the room. This not only has a physiological impact on you, it also gives you a larger presence and help you to release nervous energy. This is one of the things that makes video a critical tool in helping someone enhance his or her presentation skills. It is particularly helpful when we are working with individuals in a one-on-one situation who are not as "big" as they could be in front of a room. I often ask people I coach to totally overexaggerate their movements. I have them shake out first, to loosen up a bit, and then go big— *very* big. Of course, they feel a little silly doing this, but they are usually game to try. What invariably happens when we play back the video is that they are surprised to find that their movements do not seem overexaggerated at all; in fact, they look quite natural.

- *When sitting, make sure your arms are above the table and that your posture is slightly forward leaning, open, and erect.* Again, assume as much of your space as you can. More of your body will be in view, which will make your presence larger. This is particularly important if you have a small frame. If your hands and arms are underneath the table, it can appear as though the table is swallowing you.

- *Assuming you have time to adjust a chair's height before a meeting, do so.* If you happen upon a chair that is oddly lower than everyone else's, politely ask for another.

- *Always avoid a podium if you can.* If you stand behind it, you will become a fraction of yourself.

I strongly recommend taking 15 minutes to watch Cuddy's video. Not only is the material very compelling, but she is also a phenomenal speaker and a great example of almost every skill and concept we teach. She uses simple language, relies on simple visuals, and tells a simple story—and she delivers it with humor and personality.

CHALLENGE

Before your next big presentation (or even a small one) head to the restroom and assume a power pose. When you leave, be conscious of continuing your open stance as you get ready for your presentation (hands on hips, one arm on a wall, etc.). Go ahead and be powerful (in a nice way!).

Strategy Sessions and Rehearsals

To get to the point of a finals presentation, the selling organization has already invested significantly in things such as:

- The original marketing and sales effort that triggered the RFP
- Client meetings and research to develop intelligence
- The crafting of the RFP response
- Pricing discussions
- Technology demonstrations

This is why I am perplexed when I see organizations shortchange the preparation and rehearsal for a sales presentation; to have invested so much and to get this far and then give anything less than 100 percent does not make sense. Sometimes I will hear that a small deal does not warrant the preparation. If you don't care about winning the deal enough to be fully prepared, why would you go after the deal in the first place?

Two disciplines are required to thoroughly prepare for a finals presentation:

1. A *Strategy Session*. Feel free to call this whatever you want (some organizations call this a *dry run*). I define it as "the preparation

that is focused on the team's messaging, or the *what* we will say"
Specifically, the team is working to determine:

- The Big Three messages and how each individual component of the presentation can reinforce them
- The key messages for each topic that will be covered (the
  elements of the storyboard—key points, stories, proof
  points, language)
- The materials (handouts, slides) that will support communication of the messages
- Logistics for the rehearsal and the presentation

2. A *Rehearsal*. This is where the team actually gets the presentation
   on its feet—meaning that people rehearse in character as they will
   present (standing or sitting without notes) and receive feedback
   from the other team members. Caution: People may suggest that
   they need to work more on their messaging in an effort to avoid
   the rehearsal. They may also just want to talk *about* what they are
   going to say as opposed to rehearsing and saying it in character.
   It is natural to want to avoid rehearsing in front of peers; for some
   people, it's actually more intimidating than the actual presentation. Guard this exercise carefully, as it will have an impact on the
   team's ultimate performance. Be prepared for some pushback.
   You may hear protests like, "I am better if I don't rehearse." Be as
   supportive as you can while holding your ground.

   Be sure to rehearse and time the *entire presentation*, from the
   introductions to the close. You can stop between each section to
   provide feedback; just remember to stop the timer and take note
   of the time so that you know how long the presentation will take.

A Note on Time

Since we do not know how many questions the client will ask along
the way, it's a challenge to accurately time a presentation. But it is
always better to finish early or to leave more time for dialogue than to

run over. For this reason, I have teams time a two-hour presentation for 75 minutes—at the most. For a one-hour presentation, I have the team time the presentation for 30 minutes. It is much easier to stretch the time than to rein it in.

My firm has a very high close ratio on the deals that we coach. I would like to think that it is largely due to all the strategies and tips that I have provided in this book. I would not be honest, however, if I did not also give credit to the simple fact that the teams we coach are, by design, well prepared and well rehearsed. On large deals, our coaching often involves two full days for the entire team. The teams we coach typically win because they are up against less prepared teams. This is not because the competitor teams don't think rehearsals and preparedness are important (most know that they are). It is because they don't have the time or can't get the organizational support for this kind of commitment. Salespeople often wait until they have been officially deemed finalists to begin the preparation for the presentation—something that requires them to scramble at the last minute when the client issues a date that is just around the corner.

This is why I suggest that sales organizations *assume* that they will be selected as finalists and invited to present as soon as a deal is well qualified. This means gathering the team and scheduling strategy sessions and rehearsals *before* they are actually selected as finalists. In large organizations, where support from marketing departments and others is required, go ahead and tee them up. Make assumptions on when the finals will be held and what direction (if any) the clients will give you regarding want they want to be covered and whom they would like to attend. This approach will provide an advantage to your team off the bat, as your competition will likely wait for the invitation. The worst-case scenario in following this advice is that you will have prepared for a situation that is not going to happen. However, there's is a lot less at stake in this scenario than in going into finals without having adequately prepared.

Debrief Sessions

As important as it is to prepare before, it's equally crucial to take some time to gather the team *after* a sales presentation to debrief. There are two objectives for this debriefing session: The first is to capture the team members' insights on what they learned from the client. Given that people hear and see things differently, it is important to get everyone's perspective on follow-up and discuss any new information the group learned about the client's needs, preferences, and so forth. It is also a great opportunity to brainstorm on how to move the deal forward.

The second objective for the debrief is to assess the team's performance, specifically by asking, "What did we do well, and what ideas do we have for improvement?" I suggest using the "keep, stop, start" model commonly used in change management initiatives: "What should we *keep* doing, *stop* doing, and *start* doing?" This keeps the session positive and the feedback constructive. A sample agenda for the debrief is available in Section 5, "The Tool Kit."

If You Remember Only Three Things:

1. The client will read your team's behaviors like a book, so make sure that it reads well and that you are supporting each other throughout the presentation.
2. It is important that salespeople assume a leadership role for the team, ensuring that everyone has the information they need and that the team is coached to achieve their highest level of performance.
3. Adequate preparation and rehearsal makes and breaks deals.

Interview with Ron Hopkinson

Ron Hopkinson is a partner at prominent financial services law firm Cadwalader, Wickersham & Taft LLP, where he heads the

Private Equity Group. He has played a significant role in some of the world's largest leveraged buyouts and high-profile private equity transactions. He has also worked with leading corporations in major acquisitions, joint ventures, and corporate restructurings. The boardroom is a second home to Ron—and a place where he has seen more than his share of presentations. Following is Ron's advice to sales teams.

On creating the right dynamics from the start:

> There should always be one person running the meeting. And . . . keep the numbers of people down! I don't know what the "right" or magic number is, but it seems to be no more than five or six. A small group allows for more dialogue and more interactivity.
>
> The introductions are always a bore; instead of the usual, let your salespeople say something intelligent. People want to see the personalities. Keep the formality to a minimum.
>
> I hate the first 10 minutes of most presentations. We have to listen to some guy tell us about the firm's history and all the deals that they have done. Please put it in a handout in case we want to review it later. Or at the very least, leave it until the end.

On the importance of making it about the client:

> In this business, you don't want to feel like you're being sold to. And that is exactly what it feels like when someone comes in with a generic presentation. Give me something that is completely tailored to my problem; get to the heart of it as soon as possible and find a way to add value. Make it interactive; smart people like to talk every once in a while.

(*continued*)

(*continued*)

On keeping it dynamic and changing the game:

One of my most memorable presentations was given by a couple of scientists. The first guy got up and was clearly brilliant, but his presentation was so technical that he was losing everyone. The second guy started his part of the presentation by telling us that he speaks to a lot of different audiences, and it would be helpful for him to understand everyone's background. So we went around the room, each speaking for a few minutes. This did two things: It got everyone engaged, and it completely shifted the game by putting everyone on the spot. All of a sudden it felt like he was the professor and I was the student, because he took control of the group and kept me engaged by using the Socratic method throughout.

I think you need to change the game and make it dynamic. When you change things up so that you are in control, it doesn't feel like you are desperate for the business. It is a little bit like the girl who plays hard to get.

Analyzing Your Audience

Understanding your audience members' personalities and the overall dynamics in the room is critical to achieving a successful sales presentation. Of course, this is often easier said than done—particularly if you have limited access to the buying committee. This is when you have to employ your best Sherlock Holmes skills. Here are some tips that will help:

To every extent possible, *use coaches (sometimes fondly referred to as "moles") to help you build your intelligence.* These are usually (but not necessarily) people within the client's organization. They may take the form of previous colleagues, personal friends, administrative assistants, or champions who may have worked with you or your firm in another division.

Turn to LinkedIn, an incredible (and often underutilized) resource. Use it to research everyone on the buying committee. Check out their photos, their previous employers, and where they went to school. Find connections that you and other team members may have with buying committee members, and then use those connections to find out more. Several years ago, a book called *I'm on LinkedIn: Now What?* (by Jason Alba) hit the market. Although I have yet to read it, I think the title is clever and very reflective of what was on everyone's mind at the time—and still is today, to some extent. You are at an enormous disadvantage if you are not actively using LinkedIn. It is well worth it even if you use it only to research people for sales presentations and to catalog your contacts (which is a great feature in itself, because people update their own contact information, so you always have an updated contact list).

CHALLENGE

Go to your LinkedIn page. On the right of the home page is a list of "people you may know." Add 10 new contacts from these choices.

Alternative challenge: If you haven't yet started your LinkedIn page, do so. Invite at least 20 people to connect.

In your research, you want to uncover information that will give you insight into how the audience might interact with you and with their colleagues during the presentation. You want to learn as much as you can about the committee as a whole and the individuals who make up the committee. Following are some questions you may consider.

Information You Want to Know About the Buying Committee Dynamics

- Do they work closely together?
- Are they likely to agree?
- Are there any team dynamics of which we should be aware?
- Will they likely have many questions?
- Who is apt to have the greatest influence on the decision making?
- Does anyone have veto power?

- Who, if anyone, outside of the buying committee is likely to weigh in on the decision (senior leaders, outside counsel, consultants)?

Information You Want to Know About Each Committee Member

- How long has she been with the company? What is likely her next move?
- What is his personality (quiet or outgoing, big-picture–oriented or detailed-oriented, analytical or conceptual)?
- What's her background? Where else has she worked? What is his role now, and what has it been previously?

Some of these questions are more sensitive than others, so you obviously want to be cognizant of the relationship you have with the person providing the information and frame your questions accordingly. What you are really looking for here is insight into how this group will interact with each other and how, as individuals, they might impact the team dynamics.

Once you have this intelligence, use it wisely. Review it in your strategy session and think through the implications for how and what you present and how you engage the audience. Assess the individuals who make up the client's team and what you might expect of them. Following are some typical ways that salespeople and colleagues might describe members of a buying committee, as well as how you might strategize an approach that recognizes this insight.

- *"John is all about numbers."*

When a sales team hears this kind of feedback, their initial reaction is usually to load up with numbers. However, this may not always be the right approach, particularly if the buying committee also has members who are not all about the numbers. In this case, I often coach the team to carefully consider what information is necessary to include in the presentation and how to handle questions from the numbers guy. While each situation is different, it is sometimes a good idea to suggest that you handle detailed conversations like this either before or after the presentation. This also holds true with technology. I have seen teams panic in their attempts to conduct elaborate technology demos, all because they know there is going to be a techie in the room. But these kinds of narrow, detailed conversations have the potential to derail a presentation. Therefore, it is important to strategize ways to address individual needs while not getting too detailed for the entire group.

One way to do this is to acknowledge the individual(s) who are wired for detail up front. You may try approaches similar to these examples: "John, I know that you will need to look at these numbers in more detail after the presentation. For the purposes of today's discussion, I thought I would give an overview for the entire group, and you and I can later do a deep dive if you would like." Or, "Maryanne, if you or your team would like a more in-depth review of the technology, I am happy to put you together with our tech group. Right now, I thought it would be helpful to look at this from the user's perspective so that the group can get an idea about the experience of using it. Does that make sense?"

- *"Olivia will not say anything in the meeting, but will be very vocal afterward."*

When I hear this kind of feedback, I look for ways to engage Olivia. I assign one person on the team to specifically look out for Olivia's body language, and, while not calling her out in an obvious way, I suggest the team check in with her occasionally on her likely area of interest, saying something like, "Olivia, I know that the day-to-day relationship management is of particular importance to you. I'd love to hear your reaction to what we have reviewed so far."

The goal here is to get Olivia to voice her opinions when you are in the room, so that you can address them if necessary. Phrasing this in a way that requires Olivia to comment rather than using a yes-or-no question (e.g., "Do you have any questions or comments,

Olivia?") will provide invaluable insight into what is going on in her head—and what could potentially derail everything if she waits to express her opinions after you leave.

- *"Jamie is going to seek every opportunity to look good."*

This is a common dynamic. Jamie could be the internal guy who is overly ambitious or perhaps just insecure. He could also just be plain obnoxious by nature or the good guy who was given a bad time by his boss. Of course, the more that we know about him and his situation, the better we will be able to strategize.

There's also the possibility that Jamie is a third-party consultant.

One of my very first consulting gigs after I left Chase was *with* Chase, when I was hired to source a sales training curriculum for the company's Treasury Service Division. Even though I had worked there for years, I did not know the buying committee members who were assembled for this project. I also did not know the senior leader, who was essentially paying my invoices.

I considered myself (even then) to be a fairly confident and well-adjusted individual. Was it important to me to look good in front of this group? You bet it was! I had done a lot of work crafting the RFP, articulating the buying criteria, and identifying and qualifying vendors. This was my first consulting project, and I needed all the recognition I could get. All of my work culminated in two days of finalist presentations to the buying committee that I had assembled. A few of the vendors recognized my work in front of the buying committee. While I was more of an influencer than a decision maker in this process, it is very likely that I was probably a little more enthusiastic (consciously or unconsciously) of those who acknowledged my contribution to the process.

Having been in this position, I can tell you that it makes a *huge* difference when a presenter acknowledges your work. Whether the need for recognition is coming from a good place or a bad place, this dynamic is common—and we need to be prepared to deal with it in the sales presentation. The important thing here is to acknowledge the person who needs the recognition so that he or she doesn't feel compelled to do it him- or herself.

Just recently, I coached a team on a presentation in which a couple of consultants were involved. When I asked Tom, the salesperson, what he was most concerned about, he said that the two consultants were a little insecure and would need to look good in front of the client. He felt he better be prepared for them to drill him on the numbers. Since this prospect was less than appealing, we strategized a plan in which Tom would say in advance of the financial section, "Mark and John were instrumental in helping us understand the numbers. They worked tirelessly, making sure that we had what we needed, and they were always available so we could bounce strategies off them."

Apparently, this up-front acknowledgment was good enough for the consultants. They were quiet and supportive throughout the presentation and approached Tom as the team was leaving to congratulate him on a job well done.

- *"Everyone will take the lead from Teddy. If he is engaged, everyone else will be."*

When you know (or even just think) this dynamic is the case, it is important that you do not find yourself focusing too much on this person, thereby alienating the rest of the team. This will be transparent, and frankly annoying, to everyone present. Even when we have been told that one person will lead the decision making, the team may have more influence than even *they* think they do. And even in the case where they *don't* pull much weight, the sales team members are the last people they want to know this.

You must treat the most junior person at the table with the same level of respect as the most senior person. This means giving them equal amounts of eye contact, including them in discussions, and checking in with them occasionally.

Several years ago, I was helping a client source a partner to help with a branding project. My client had recently hired a young go-getter who would act as project manager. Sarah was young (and looked even younger) and attractive. I know what you're thinking: young and beautiful—what a curse! Right? Well, it actually *can* be. Maybe not a curse, but definitely a disadvantage in a business setting, particularly when you are also quiet, which is true of Sarah.

My client and I watched one team after another present to us, totally ignoring Sarah the entire time. They probably assumed she was an intern with no authority or influence on the decision, which was a big mistake, because Sarah actually had *a lot* of influence. We respected her opinion in this decision, and we were very conscious of how the sales teams interacted with her. As project manager, she needed to be working with people who would respect her at the get-go.

While treating everyone with the same amount of respect may sound like motherhood and apple pie, I cannot tell you how often I hear this criticism of sales teams when I debrief clients on their presentation experiences. And if you have ever been the person whom the sales team (or any team, for that matter) has deemed unimportant, you know how distressing it feels.

- *"Donna is likely to be disruptive; she wants to be center stage."*

We all know the type. Because the amateur psychiatrist in me immediately labels this as a sign of insecurity, my job is to help Donna feel secure. I do this by acknowledging her role, checking in with her frequently, and giving her credit when I can ("As Donna said, this factor is critical to success"). Chances are that Donna has this reputation with the buying committee as well. In this case, it is not uncommon for the other members to jump in to help control Donna.

Okay, that covers some of the types of people you might find in the room, but what about the ones who are *not* attending, either by design or because they have a conflict? It is important to think about them as well. I suggest calling your client contact and saying something like this: "We are looking forward to the presentation tomorrow, and I wanted to check in on the attendees. Are there any changes or any decision makers who cannot make the meeting?" If the answer is yes, find out who cannot attend and what their role is. Then continue, "I am happy to spend some time with that individual separately, if that would be helpful. I would also like to put together a set of materials that are a little bit more comprehensive, since that person will not be attending the meeting."

It is possible that you will not get much from this; however, it's also possible that you will gain insight into the decision-making process and create an opportunity to connect with a decision maker that your competition will not, which could be a significant advantage to you. If you do provide materials, the people receiving them will likely appreciate it if you include a handwritten note and an invitation to call to review them, if necessary.

It is also important to remember that there are frequently decision makers whom we don't even know about. This makes it all the more important to have an easily retold story that can live beyond the presentation.

Thinking through all the decision makers will help to ensure that you are covering all bases. Planning for those in the room will help to guard against someone throwing the presentation off track.

If You Remember Only Three Things:

1. Gather as much intelligence on the client team members as possible before the sales presentation.
2. Plan in advance for challenging personalities and meeting dynamics.
3. Don't forget about the people not attending. Create a plan for them as well.

The Materials: What We Say It With

11

Dodging the Bullets: Avoiding Death by PowerPoint

Myth: The deck is the presentation.
Truth: You are the presentation.

How many times have you heard someone say, "I can't make it to your presentation. Can you send me your slides?" In this way, the *presentation* and the presentation *deck* have become synonymous. There is a general perception that if someone misses the presentation, he or she can make up for it by reviewing the slides.

But here's a news flash: Slides are meant to *support*—not *replace*—the speaker. If someone can fully understand the presentation by simply reviewing the slides, then there is something wrong with the slides, or perhaps there never should have been a presentation to begin with. As I have said many times, the presentation is often the only chance that the sales team has to connect with the decision makers. If the presentation is all about the slides, it distracts from you. *You* are the presentation.

By now, "death by PowerPoint" is almost a household phrase. It is fascinating to me that we continue to abuse this application in spite of the commonly voiced complaints:

- There's way too much text on slides.
- It's painful to watch people read from it.

- There are too many bullet points!
- Charts and tables can't be deciphered.
- You can't see if from the back of the room!
- It's *boring*!

We relate to all of this because we are not only presenters, we are often audience members (or victims) as well. And deep down inside, we know that the problem has nothing to do with PowerPoint itself. It has to do with the people using PowerPoint.

Why, when we know it is not working, do we keep creating the same slides and doing the same thing?

There are a number of reasons, and understanding them is the first step to breaking the old PowerPoint mold once and for all.

"I know you can't read this but..."

Reason #1: *"We have always done it this way."* People are particularly resistant to change when the stakes are high, especially when they have experienced success doing it the old way. Let's face it, change can be scary—even more so when it involves standing up in front of people presenting. Add this to the fact that the sales presentation may mean a lot of money to you or may have an impact on your career or, worse, your reputation. The reality of the situation is that most salespeople have been successful not because of but *in spite of* poor presentation skills. They get comfortable doing it the way they have always done it—and this includes using the familiar slide format, with a headline followed by a series of bullet points with too many words on each line. Or maybe you use a graph or chart that you know people can't see, but it seems to be okay if you preface it with, "I know you can't see this, but . . ."

Reason #2: *"I am not quite sure we* want *to be different."* I have observed that some businesspeople are actually quite fearful of being different, which is somewhat ironic considering that salespeople and teams are always searching for differentiation. This dichotomy hit me hard when I was coaching a team presenting to a top pharmaceutical company. We had just worked with the sales organization to completely redesign their deck—and I mean *completely*. The sales force put up significant resistance as it was rolled out, which is understandable, because it was a departure from anything that they had worked with before. When helping prepare the team for this presentation—one of the first times they were using the new deck—one salesperson politely asked me, "Do you really think that it is a good idea to have a presentation that is so different from what the competition will be presenting?" She went on to explain that she was concerned that it might somehow throw the client off. I answered her question by telling her that I thought it was a *great* idea to be different. I went on to explain that *how* the team presents can be a great opportunity to provide a distinctive and memorable experience, one that will really set the team apart from the competition. And, given the commoditized industry in which this particular team worked, their presentation was one way to answer the client's inevitable (but sometimes silent) question: "What makes you different?"

Unfortunately, my words did not seem to have much impact. This salesperson pulled me aside the following day to show me a presentation she had somehow wrangled from the prospect's organization.

It was a typical corporate presentation loaded with line after line of bullet points. She asked me, "If they used this in their own organization, how are they going to feel about something so different?" My response was, "Probably relieved." I asked which she would prefer if she were a member of the audience: to listen to someone read bullets from a slide or to hear someone tell a story supported by highly engaging images and keywords? She responded, "Well, when you put it that way . . ."

While I am not sure I convinced her that day, I am pleased to tell you that she has since become one of the greatest champions of the new presentation style. Sometimes you need to experience the success of a new behavior before you are ready to own it.

Reason #3: *"We don't have time to fix it."* Addressing bad Power-Point slides takes time, effort, and finesse. Most sales teams are hustling at the last minute. Sometimes this is due to factors outside of a sales team's control, and sometimes it is due to poor time management. We live in a high-pressure world, with more than enough responsibilities to fill our days. As a result, we usually end up addressing those things that are forced to the top of our priority list by time pressure. In the heat of a deal, people want to focus on a presentation's content, not its design. Unfortunately, I have found that the team is frequently so busy fine-tuning the deck (changing this word here, that bullet point there) that they do not take a moment to step back and look at the slide's design. They rarely reserve time to ask themselves: "Does this communicate what I need it to? Does this support my point and my message? Will this maintain my ability to connect with the audience, or will it distract from me?"

Reason #4: *"Design is not for businesspeople."* In other words, "We are about the important stuff—the numbers, the solutions, and the deal. The design is the fluff that we can leave to marketing, communications, and creative people who do it for a living."

However, it seems that there has been a greater focus on the power of design over the past decade or so. I expect one of the reasons may have to do with Apple and Steve Jobs. *Cool*, *sleek*, *elegant*, and *simple* are all words that come to mind when I think of the crystal-clear glass, chrome boarders, backlit keyboard, and stylish logos that are Apple's hallmark. While Apple's product design intent is more than aesthetic, I think most of us would say we like the way these products look.

Another example of the power of modern design is Google. The search page, which is as familiar to most of us as our living rooms, is wonderfully clutter-free. The colorful and sometimes decorated logo sits in a sea of white space, along with a rectangular box and two buttons, one labeled "Google search" and the other labeled "I'm feeling lucky." When you think about it, there is probably no more valuable real estate on the planet than the Google home page, yet it consistently remains free of advertisements. I often project a screenshot of the Google page in workshops and ask my audience what it communicates. The adjectives always involve terms like *simple*, *creative*, and *fun*. The consistency in these messages is not happenstance; it is by design. Google knows that its design has a strong voice, and it is used very deliberately and consciously to tell the world who the company is and what it stands for.

Garr Reynolds is the author of a best-selling book on presentation design called *Presentation Zen*. His popular blog, www.presentationzen .com, is filled with great tips and examples of the good, the bad, and the ugly. I encourage you to check out his blog and/or book. The following quote from Reynolds sums up his view that each one of us is responsible for understanding the impact of design on our world: "Design is a big, big deal. We all have a responsibility to understand its potential and its power. You do not need to be a designer—but you do need to become more design sensitive or 'design mindful.'"

Businesspeople who think that design does not matter are at a disadvantage—because they are likely to be unconscious of or choose to ignore the messages that their design is sending. Remember, just because you do not deliberately *set out* to communicate something doesn't mean that you are not sending messages. Ask yourself, "What messages do my material's design send about me and my firm?"

CHALLENGE

Pull out your last sales presentation deck. Focusing just on the design, not the content, ask yourself, "What messages did the design send to this client? Are these the messages I want to send?

Reason #5: *"The slides are a crutch to help me to remember what to say."* People who have been presenting with a traditional corporate deck find comfort in having a lot of words on the slide—since these often help them remember what to say. Hopefully, they are not reading from the slide (although sometimes they do, and we all know how terrible that is—ugh). We have found in most cases that they really don't need *all* the words; usually, they know their material cold. If you take their slides away and ask about a particular capability or process, they can easily and very naturally talk about it. (Of course, there is a larger problem if a presenter cannot do this. You shouldn't bring people in front of the client unless they know their stuff cold.)

Can people read and listen at the same time? Think about it. Have you ever been reading a book only to realize that you have comprehended nothing of the last two paragraphs because your attention was tuned in to the conversation next to you? Or perhaps you were discussing a document with someone and asked for a minute so that you could read a couple of lines. Maybe you have been on a conference call and found yourself distracted by an incoming e-mail, and you didn't realize that you had totally tuned out of the conversation—until someone asked you to comment.

It is physically impossible for most of us to read and listen at the same time. Why do we ask our audiences to do so? We would be better off asking them to jump on one foot and chew gum at the same time. In fact, they might at least be able to listen while they do that!

When faced with a choice between listening and reading a slide, research tells us that the audience is more likely to read. Not only does this get in the way of our chance to connect with them, but their ability to listen (which is not great to begin with) is hampered as they look back and forth between you and the slide.

Reason #6: *"We don't know how to fix it."* With all of the reasons leading up to this, it may seem quite overwhelming. It is hard to determine where to begin and how to get the job done. If you are a member of a large organization where many people are using a standard presentation, you will inevitably get some pushback. Change calls people out of their comfort zone. You have two choices here: You can do a total overhaul, or you can make changes intermittently. Your level of urgency—and the resources available to you—will determine the best approach. Whether you go full steam ahead or take small steps, you need to start with the question, "Where do we begin?"

Fixing the presentation requires both right- and left-brain thinking, and some of us are better at this than others. If this is not your forte, find someone who has a talent for it, or at least make sure you engage both right- and left-brain thinkers in the exercise. It is hard to focus on both at the same time, so don't even attempt to. Review each slide for content, then review it for design.

Another option is to outsource the project, provided you have the budget for it. Find three or four designers and ask for samples of their work. Do not assume because they are in the business that they know how to create powerful slides specific to a sales presentation. Be careful about hiring an advertising agency for this. I have found that some agencies tend to produce slides and stories that look like advertisements—and we know by now that sales presentations require a more personal form of messaging. Slogan-like phrasing does not belong in a sales presentation; it can often feel impersonal and disingenuous, which can cause the audience to feel as though they are being sold to. If you outsource, make sure that the company you hire *really* understands the nuts and bolts of sales.

Where to Start

Now that we have analyzed many of the reasons that we become stuck in a pattern of death by PowerPoint, how can we start to get *un*stuck? It all begins with the right frame of mind and knowing that making a change is worth it. Altering an ingrained behavior and approach is an uphill battle, which is why so many sales teams have not changed their approach. Keep in mind that changing how you present is an opportunity for you to be different and to create a competitive advantage. Dare to be different. Go big or go home. And kick off the process by taking the following steps.

The Ruthless Screening

Part A. Analyze Once you are committed to fixing the problem, you can start by analyzing your existing presentation deck by putting it through a ruthless screening.

1. Gather some team members, and *analyze the presentation* by answering the following questions:
   - Overall, what messages does the presentation currently convey?
   - To what extent does it allow you to tell the story from the client's perspective?
   - Does it support or distract from the presenter's connection with the audience?
   - Is it in plain English, or does it contain industry jargon and acronyms?
   - Is it visually appealing?
   - What do the choices of color and font communicate? (Think simple versus complicated, traditional versus modern, elegant versus tacky, boring versus interesting, typical versus different, current versus stodgy.)
   - What do the choices of images convey? Are they elegant and high-quality, or cheesy and clip-arty?

- To what extent does it look and feel like every other competitor's presentation?
- What do the headlines communicate? Are they original and to the point, or self-serving, meaningless corporate-speak?
- Do graphs and charts clearly communicate what you want them to, or do they require binoculars and a lengthy explanation to get to the point?

2. Based on your analysis, *determine what, if any, components you should preserve.* It will often be the case that you are better off simply clearing the deck and starting with a blank slate.
3. *Capture your intent.* What is the one overriding message that you want this presentation to convey to *every* audience? (See Chapter 3, "Develop a Story.")
4. If you have the budget, *hire the expertise.* If not, follow Part B.

Part B. Plan   *Create a storyboard.* Using the same technique discussed in Chapter 3, create a storyboard for the standard presentation. This process will initially require your left-brain, logical thinking. What is the logical flow for the presentation from the *client's* perspective? What key messages do you want to convey in each section of the presentation? How will you weave your value proposition throughout? What proof points and stories can you incorporate?

1. *Determine the look and feel for the slides.*
   - What *colors and fonts* best support your message?
   - What *images* are important to include?
2. *Design the slides.* This is where the right-brain thinking comes in. For each slide, ask yourself:
   - What is the *one message* that you want to convey? What is the headline for that message (see headlines on page 146)?
   - What image could you use to drive home your point?
   - What (if any) *words other than the headline* might you need?

Whether you outsource this process or decide to build your deck internally, the following are some best practices to keep in mind.

Myth: The fewer the slides, the better.

Truth: Use as many slides as it takes to tell your story in an interesting and engaging way.

I am absolutely dumbfounded by the obsession people have with the number of slides in a presentation. When we sit with a team to review a presentation deck, more often than not someone will ask, "How many slides does it have?" If I had a dollar for every time I have heard someone excitedly exclaim, "I got the presentation down to *X* slides!" I would have enough money to buy an expensive new pair of shoes. These people have usually taken information that once needed 25 slides and crammed it into something like 20 slides. More often than not, they have done so *without* eliminating any content. Time and again, I hear the familiar refrain, "We can get rid of this slide if we combine it with the one before." Of course, this is all done with the best of intentions; most people are thinking, "We don't want to bore our audiences with hundreds of slides."

Ironically, however, the *number* of slides is typically not the problem. When it is the problem, there are usually too *few* slides—not too many. No, this is not a typo. I actually wrote that people often make the mistake of having too *few* slides, not too many. Here's why:

- A slide is meant to *support one idea*, not multiple ideas. As we discussed earlier, we want the audience members to focus on you, not on the slide. We want them listening and connecting, not reading and processing.

- *Our world's current pace is faster than ever before.* Technology has allowed us to communicate in a much more visual way than we have in the past. Think about the difference between the Pac-Man of the 1980s and the video games that your children (or you) may be enjoying today. Notice how much is going on visually the next time you watch CNN or think about YouTube's extraordinary success as a communication vehicle. Consider as well how websites have evolved over the past 10 years. Even our phones are more visual.

Now, think about the typical presentation approach in which a presenter sits on a text-heavy slide for five minutes. In most cases, this has not changed since PowerPoint began replacing slides and transparencies in the early 1990s.

A visually appealing presentation that reminds the audience of key points and uses color and images to foster emotion will keep an audience's attention. Each time the presenter moves from one slide to the next, it reconnects the audience to the message and reinforces the key points. When an audience member's listening wavers (and this will always happen, no matter how fascinating you are), he or she can easily glance to the slide to reconnect.

When I work with companies to redesign their decks, I know I need to brace myself for the sales force's inevitable resistance to the number of slides and the brief content on each. Fortunately, I also know that once they are educated on the rationale behind it and have experience using it, they will become great champions of the approach.

About a year ago, a client hired our firm to completely revamp its sales presentation approach. We worked on this company's stake-in-the-ground story, created a master deck, trained the sales force and various other team members, and then provided deal coaching on the first few deals. To say the sales force resisted this new approach is an understatement. It happened that the first deal to which they would apply all of this was a very large one—the largest client that they would have if they won the business. The stakes were high, and the emotions were raw. The sales manager mandated the use of the new deck; had she not, this team would never have agreed to use it.

The sales presentation was scheduled to last 90 minutes, so we planned for one hour of presentation time. The deck that the team would present contained 81 slides. There was so much pushback that I did not think the team would ever get past the fact that there were 81 slides—but God bless them, they did. They practiced and then presented all 81 slides, while following the planned timeline.

The team returned to the hotel after the presentation for a debrief—and they were elated. They told me that one of the buying committee members walked them out and said that, although he could not be certain of the outcome, their presentation was the best by far. They were incredibly proud of their performance—as they should have been. They became champions of the approach going forward. In fact, they were even asked to re-create their performance for an internal audience.

When I introduce the idea of using more slides rather than fewer during my workshops, I often stop and ask my audience, "During the two hours that we have been together, has anyone in the room thought, 'Wow, she is presenting a lot of slides?'" They usually chuckle and respond, "No, I guess not." I then ask them to guess how many slides I have shown them, and they generally suggest about a third of the number that I have actually used. They are surprised when I put my presentation in slide-sorter view to reveal the actual number. I have learned that the audience is not aware of the number of slides when there are very few words on each slide and they are highly visual. It is a little like being aware of the number of pixels in a photograph: You don't even notice them, because you are more involved in looking at the picture as a whole.

Salespeople appreciate this approach greatly once it's up and running, because it limits a lot of the deck drama often associated with preparing for a presentation (e.g., people changing this word on slide 8 and adding that bullet point on slide 6). This approach allows you to limit the customization of the deck to the following three activities:

1. *Creating* the initial slide(s) that outlines your understanding of the client's needs
2. *Eliminating* slides that are not relevant
3. *Creating* the "If we can leave you with only three things" slide (this is the ending slide, the one that captures in plain, punchy language the Big Three messages that you want to leave the client with)

> **deck drama** \'dek drah-muh\ *n.* The time-wasting activity that occurs in the final days of preparation for a sales presentation that distracts the members of the team from the important task of developing a compelling story for the client; RELATED WORDS: "wordsmith," "death by PowerPoint," "time-waster"

Myth: The more detail we include, the smarter we look.

Truth: "Simplicity is the ultimate sophistication" (Leonardo da Vinci).

I remember when my sons were in grade school, they brought home one paper after another with the comment, "Add more detail!" written across the top. Their teachers considered detail to be a good thing (and lack of it a bad thing). Likewise, being detail-oriented is an important criterion for our first jobs; it can be a ticket to the fast track early in our careers. However, at some point in our development as leaders, we need to begin to let go of our attention to detail and let someone else worry about it. After all, who wants a CEO or president who is all about the details? While many details lie behind any complex sale, when it is time for the sales presentation, it is time to present our offering in a simple and sophisticated manner that will make our recommendation concrete without getting mired in detail.

Animation

If you happen to be a whiz at all the animation tricks that are available to you on PowerPoint, I would like to suggest that you forget everything that you learned. For the most part, animation is unnecessary and distracting. It may occasionally be helpful to present a list or a number that you want to hold back from the audience. If this is the case, avoid using the "fly in, peek in, rise up, shimmer, wave, blink, fade out, fly out" options. Keep it simple, and use only the "appear" function. While this instruction may seem to conflict with my earlier assertion that we need to keep the presentation visually interesting, this suggestion has a lot to do with who is in the driver's seat. If you hire a professional who really *understands* design, then by all means incorporate sophisticated movement and animation in your design. Otherwise, these fancy capabilities can be dangerous in the hands of the mere mortal.

Slide Headlines

The typical slide headlines state *what is* on the slide, not *why* it is important. For example, a standard slide about technology might have a headline that reads: WEB-BASED TOOLS. Underneath it, there might be some screen shots of those web-based tools. I would prefer to see a headline that tells me *what the client should take away* from the discussion on web-based tools. Is it that they are state-of-the-art? Second to none? As easy as it gets? Carefree? Personalized? Slide headlines should state in plain, punchy language the point of the slide. Ask yourself, "What is my message?" When it is a declarative statement, I like to use punctuation, since it brings punch to your statement and drives the point home. For instance, the reason that these web-based tools are so great is because "We make it simple."

Following are some examples of strong slide headlines.

- We take care of it all (so you don't have to).
- We get you!
- We are committed to you.
- We are number one in customer service.
- We expect 10 percent growth.
- We provide extraordinary service.
- More people prefer X than Y.
- We have this down.
- We guarantee it.
- Our clients appreciate us.
- We deliver results.
- We've got a track record to prove it.

Client Logos

In their efforts to be client-focused, I have seen a few sales teams incorporate the client's brand into their marketing materials by mirroring the client company's colors and adding its logo. While I completely support a focus on the client, I also like to remind people that it is important to maintain *your* identity and *your* brand. You are separate and distinct from your prospects—that's why they are hiring you. It's appropriate to incorporate their logos on the cover slide of your presentations and perhaps in slides that refer specifically to them (rather than using their name); however, you don't want to overdo it. And, of course, *always* request permission from a prospect company's marketing and communications department before using its logo—and be sure to abide by all the guidelines.

It is very common to see a slide template that has the client's and the selling company's logo running across the bottom or the top of all slides as a footer or header. I find this to be unnecessary and distracting clutter that takes away from the message. There's a bigger problem if the client or the sales team needs to be reminded on every slide who is presenting or to whom they are presenting!

In fact, one of the craziest slide presentations I have ever seen was from a small financial advisory practice. In addition to breaking all the rules (or following all the rules that were meant to be broken), every header and footer was loaded up with all its affiliations, its website address, telephone number, and mailing address. Yes, all of this was on *every single slide*. It was as if the presenters expected the clients to whip out their phones in the midst of their presentation, go to their website, call their office, or MapQuest their location. What were they thinking? These were smart people! The reality of the situation is that they were *not* thinking about the design—because they were too busy focusing on the content. They made the common mistake of failing to understand the power of design.

A Picture Is Worth a Thousand Words

Let's face it, pictures are a lot more interesting to look at than words, particularly on a large screen. Not only are they more interesting, but an image can foster stronger emotions and communicate messages better than almost any well-crafted sentence, paragraph, or manuscript. Advertisers and marketers understand this, which is why brochures, commercials, and well-designed websites contain photographs (thank God, since the world would be a pretty boring place without them). The same holds true for the sales presentation: A boardroom that has a slide show without pictures is just that—a bored room! (Corny? Yes. But true? *Absolutely.*)

I like to use images for two reasons:

1. They foster emotion.
2. They can drive home a critical point—and therefore bolster one of your Big Three messages.

When I think about the emotive power of an image, I think of the famous "Miracle on Ice," the photo that captured the miraculous victory of the U.S. hockey team over the Soviet team in 1980. You have to smile when you see that one. On the other side of the spectrum, I think about the ASPCA commercial that is accompanied by the Sarah McLachlan song. . . . Well, I could cry just typing this.

In my presentation on the power of image to foster emotion, I project a slide of an adorable laughing baby. My point to the group is that you would have to be inhuman *not* to smile when you see this picture. And we want our audiences smiling during in the sales presentation. Maybe not with *every* slide they see, but images can be a low-risk way to incorporate a little levity. Similarly, when it is time for a role-play during our sales training workshops, I project a whimsical picture of a greyhound dog with sunglasses and a scarf wrapped around her head and over one shoulder. It is particularly powerful because I project it when people are a little stressed about the prospect of role-playing (and really, who isn't?). I do not expect the image to spur my participants to start rolling over laughing, but it *does* make them smile—and I figure the more often that we can do that, the better.

The same holds true in the sales presentation. Why not have an image of a child trying to drink from a fire hydrant if you are trying to communicate that people are overloaded with information? How about using an image of a duck with an open wingspan protecting her ducklings from the rain as a backdrop for a conversation about risk?

There have been several occasions when we have been working with a deal team where we've incorporated an image to emphasize one of our key messages. One example that stands out was a presentation to a client who was potentially leaving a provider because the client company was not getting the personal attention it wanted. The other competitor was a very small firm, and one of its three big messages was, "We are the right fit—not too big, not too small, but just right." As you might imagine, as a backdrop to this message, we found an image of three rocking chairs that looked like they were right out of "Goldilocks."

Another example is a presentation we made to a company with whom the selling firm had done business many years before. We received intelligence that it was only as a courtesy that the client company included the selling firm in the search process. The client reps figured that they had already been there, done that with the company I was coaching—and that they would likely go with someone different this time. The hurdle in this case was to demonstrate some newness. At the end of the presentation, the facilitator projected an image of a 1968 Oldsmobile, accompanied by this statement: "While we have had the opportunity to work with you in the past, I hope that through our discussion today we demonstrated that we are not your grandfather's Oldsmobile."

The most important thing to remember about using images is to make sure that they are high-quality and visually appealing. Please, please, *please*—no matter what images you choose—do not use clip art. It communicates that you are unprofessional, lazy, and cheap. You have a much better choice with the plethora of affordable stock photography that's readily available online. The rights to use many images for the purposes of a sales presentation can be purchased for under $10. My favorite site to purchase images is www.istockphoto.com (other sites are www.shutterstock.com and www.gettyimages.com).

CHALLENGE

Think about a message that you often need to communicate to clients. Brainstorm three or four images that would support this. Be creative! Go to www.istock.com or a similar site and search images. Select the best and use them the next time you need to communicate an important message to a client.

Representing the Numbers

I'll admit it: I have never been particularly good with numbers. My eyes tend to glaze over when I am faced with a detailed spreadsheet, Excel sheet, or numbers graph. This was once my dirty little secret. As a member of the financial services industry, I was intimidated for many years by all those math geniuses with whom I often rubbed shoulders. I have since come to realize that my weakness has a silver lining, particularly when coaching for a sales presentation: I am the lowest common denominator! You may be thinking, "Well, that is an acceptable approach to pitch to bunch of human resources or marketing people, but the numbers need to be sophisticated if you have a group of distinguished actuaries." However, I recommend that your pitch should be aimed toward people at my level *at all times*—even when you have a math-savvy audience. When you talk numbers in the sales presentation, you want your message to be crystal clear. You want to have done the math, analyzed the graph, and interpreted the data *for* everyone in the room. You don't want *them* to have to figure it out; you just want to give them the punch line. If you are presenting to someone like me, you don't want me sitting there trying to discern what the heck the numbers mean—because at that point you will lose me. And even if you are presenting to a math-savvy group, you don't want them diving in and gobbling up the numbers—because you will lose them, too.

There is a time and place for all you numbers people to do your thing, but it just isn't during the sales presentation. I am not saying that the numbers are not critical. If you are looking for venture capital, you can be sure that investors will scour your numbers. If you are selling your company, you know that absolutely everyone has to do due diligence. However, it's best to analyze the prospectus outside this situation. The sales presentation is about bringing people together to hear a compelling story. Having said this, keep in mind what I said in Chapter 6: When numbers are presented with impact, they can be a powerful backdrop to your story.

Common Mistakes When Representing the Numbers—and How to Fix Them

Mistake #1. Using a Graph when You Really Don't Need One Some people have a tendency to think that any numbers you present must show up in a pie chart, a bar chart, or on an X-axis. Again, the last thing you want the audience doing when you are presenting (and attempting to connect with them) is trying to figure out what the chart says. Sometimes you just don't need one. Ask yourself these three questions when determining whether you do or do not need a chart:

1. Is the *data compelling*?
2. What is the *main point* that I want to get across to the audience?

3. Do I *really need to use a graph* or chart to communicate the point? Will it make it easier (or harder) for my audience members to grasp the most crucial information?

We typically use graphs and charts for comparison or to show how data changes over time. If your point does not need to convey either of these, then you probably don't need a chart. For example, if your point is that you retain 96 percent of your clients, you may want to simply state that. If you have determined that you *do* in fact need a graph or a chart, select the right one for your message. There are bar charts, stepped charts, Gantt charts, line charts, scatter diagrams, bubble charts, and the list goes on. For a sales presentation, you are likely to need only one or two: the bar chart and/or the pie chart.

If you choose to present a number outside of a chart—give it some authority. Make it *huge* and exciting! In the following example, no one would be able to miss the fact that this organization has a 96 percent retention rate.

If you use a bar chart, make it simple. The audience would need to glance at the following for only a few seconds to get the point that the response rate is higher when you call people on their cell phones (please, just don't call me!).

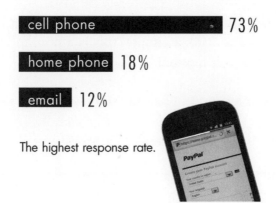

cell phone 73%

home phone 18%

email 12%

The highest response rate.

Pie charts (like real pies!) are best when the slices are not too thin. In the following example, it was not necessary to show how much each business invested in technology. The important point is that *this* business invested more than all others—keeping it simple and creating a pie that shows "Us" versus all other competitors combined.

We seriously invest in technology.

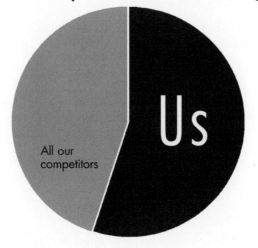

Us

All our
competitors

When creating graphs and charts to be projected on a screen, challenge yourself to be a minimalist. Ask yourself, "What is the least amount of information I can chart in order to get my point across clearly and succinctly?"

Mistake #2. Using a Headline That Labels the Graph instead of Telling the Message For example, this is a headline that tells the viewer what the graph represents:

Asian Large Corporate Banking Market Penetration

This one highlights the message you want to tell:

We are the leader in Asia.

The name of the chart, or even the research effort, is *not* what we want the audience to remember. We want them to remember that *we are the leader in Asia.*

Mistake #3. Providing Too Much Information Sometimes people are compelled to include *all* the information that is provided to them from a study or a survey. Don't include any information that isn't relevant to your point—unless, of course, it is mandated by the author of that study or report.

Mistake #4. Jumping in to Tell Your Audience About a Chart or Graph without a Setup Remember, when you're presenting a graph or a chart, while you have seen it many times, the audience is seeing it for the first time. Walk them through the setup. For example, "The following chart shows the price of services over the past 10 years. The left axis shows price, from $1 million to $10 million, and the bottom axis represents time, from 2002 to 2012. The red line is accounting services, and the green line is legal services." Then tell them what it says: "You will see that . . ."

Mistake #5. Making Assertions That You Cannot Back Up I mention this last, as I think it is obvious for most of us; however, this is probably the most important point of all. If you make an assertion, you better be able to back it up—and it should *not* be manipulated to make it something that it is not. I will be the first one to suggest that you should combine two numbers to make them more attractive: For example, "97 percent of clients rated our service very good to excellent" is both cleaner and more positive than "84 percent rated our service very good" or "13 percent rated us excellent." But it goes without saying that the numbers *have to be real*. Similarly, if you say you are "number one in the league tables," then you better be number one!

CHALLENGE

Pull out a few of your slides containing numbers. Ask yourself these questions:

- What is the point?
- What is the best way of getting the point across?
- How can I simplify the message to make it abundantly clear?

Protecting the Deck

When working with organizations to improve their presentation deck, I am always thinking about ways that our work can be protected once it is completed.

Many of our clients are Fortune 500 companies with large marketing departments that dictate the look and feel of the presentation materials to ensure alignment with the corporate brand. Therefore, the level of control that a sales team can have varies. In many organizations, salespeople and other presenters are given quite a bit of latitude in changing the content and sometimes even the design of the slides. This often results in dozens of versions of a presentation, with no quality control and very little resemblance to the original. We have seen individual team members in other organizations customize their dedicated slides to such an extent that the final product looks like a presentation that has been cobbled together in a rather disorganized way. In fact, it can be so extreme that it often appears as though three or four different organizations are presenting together. Since sales teams tend to focus on the content and not on the design, this kind of error is often overlooked. Once you have a new standard slide deck, it is important to protect it, while at the same time providing processes to allow for its improvement over time. The good news about having text-light slides is that you customize what *you* say, not what the slide says—once again, eliminating a great deal of deck drama.

The process that you establish to protect your deck depends, of course, on the size of your organization and where the deck is housed. We recently worked with a large organization to set up a deck improvement process that encouraged people to send in suggestions for improvements regularly. Each quarter, the suggestions are reviewed, changes made, and the improved deck made available.

If you are going to go to the trouble of changing your deck, be sure to put processes and standards in place to protect the original integrity of design, while at the same time allowing it to improve over time.

If You Remember Only Three Things:

1. *Slides and other visuals are meant to* support *—not* replace *—the presenter.* Make sure that your slides are designed to support the connections between the speaker and the audience.
2. *Design matters.* It sends a very strong message about who you are. Make certain that the design of your materials sends the message that you want it to.
3. *Make certain each slide has a single point* that you clearly and simply communicate.

Interview with Ian Ashken, Vice Chairman and CFO, Jarden Corporation

Ian Ashken is vice chairman and chief financial officer of Jarden Corporation, a leading provider of a diverse range of consumer products with a portfolio of more than 100 trusted, quality brands including Bicycle playing cards, Coleman, Marmot, K2, Mr. Coffee, and Rawlings. As both the vice chairman and CFO, Ian is a regular on the client side of sales presentations. Here are some of his nuggets of insight on the good, the bad, and the ugly.

On *what* to present:

We spend so much time politely listening to [information] we already know. For example, [almost all banks] who present FX hedges and derivatives to us lead with the background of the market. I hear so many presentations on the market that I am probably better equipped to tell *them* about the market!

Bring something different to us. We are on the receiving end of M&A ideas all the time—and they are more often than not all the same. Lead with your best ideas to capture our attention early—otherwise, you will just lose our interest. Then, make sure you close strong.

Above all, don't try to sell something you are not proud of; if you are selling me a glass, I don't want to find that it will shatter in my hand. I always remember a person who takes the time to evaluate what we are looking for, and admits it when he knows it isn't right for us by saying, "This isn't suitable for you." That [is someone] I will remember, and [choose to] see again.

On *how* to present:

Do something unexpected—particularly in the middle of the presentation—to get people's attention. It could be as mundane as a question about soccer . . . [just anything that] makes you wonder, "Why are they asking me this question?"

(continued)

(*continued*)

One memorable situation involved a company [that] we were considering buying. [About halfway through their presentation] to us, they took out a baseball and started throwing it around. There was some relevancy, as we manufacture baseballs. But you can't have your head in a BlackBerry if someone is throwing a baseball at you!

We were recently sitting in a meeting where about 10 or 15 people from an investment bank were presenting to us. If we asked a question for which there was not an immediate answer, like, "What is the 10-year average of these?" the person presenting would respond by saying, "We have to get back to you on that." They must have had someone in the back of the room finding out the answers, because later in the presentation a slide would pop up with the question that was asked . . . and the answer. While it was a little gimmicky, it sent the message that they were responsive and on top of things.

On sending materials ahead of time:

If you send material ahead of time, do not [presume that people] have read it. *Check.* If I have not read it, I want them to give me an overview. If I have read it, I do not want to be brought through it like I haven't.

The Strategy behind the Materials

The materials that you select to support you in telling your story can have a profound effect on the experience that you create for your audience. When we conduct presentation workshops, people frequently ask questions like these:

- Should we use PowerPoint?
- Should we project our slides?
- Should we use handouts? If so, should we give them out before or after the presentation?
- What about iPads?

When people ask about using PowerPoint, they usually just mean, "Should we project our slides somehow?" Of course, the answer to this depends on the situation. This book focuses on the conclusion of a sales cycle—the part of the process that typically ends in a so-called beauty contest in which a few finalists are presenting to client teams often composed of four or more people. In more cases than not, it is appropriate to project slides that will make it easy for the audience to follow your points and for you to control the meeting. Earlier on in the sales cycle, the meetings include much more dialogue—with the client doing the majority of the speaking. So projecting slides would be inappropriate during that stage, as it would hinder the sales team's ability to get the client talking—which is essential in developing a thorough understanding of the client's needs.

Outlined here are some pros and cons of projecting your PowerPoint.

Projecting PowerPoint Slides

Pros	Cons
Can drive home points by clearly stating what you want the audience to take away from the discussion throughout the presentation	Deadly if not used appropriately
Can use images and graphics to help an audience understand the message	Requires strong design that supports and doesn't distract from the speaker
Can make a presentation visually interesting and entertaining	Requires skill and practice to use effectively
Allows presenter to keep control of the presentation's content	Need a backup plan in case of technology challenges
Makes it easier for an audience member whose listening has lagged to get back in	
Easier to control large audiences	

As we discussed in Chapter 11, PowerPoint can be incredibly powerful when you use strong and colorful words and images as a backdrop to underscore what a speaker is saying. However, it *does* require some skill to use this tool effectively.

Slide Advancers

I am on personal mission to get slide advancers into the hands of everyone who is ever in front of a projector—because it drives me *crazy* when I see presenters depending on someone else to change their slides for them. It distracts the audience, and it takes the control and power away from the speaker right at the point he or she needs power and control *most*. If you do not have one, please get one. They cost about $30. I have found that the simpler the design, the better. You need only three buttons: one to move the slides forward, one to move them back, and one to set the screen blank. Slide advancers with a USB port are the easiest; you can just pop them into any computer and they're ready to go.

Presenter Tools

A little-known secret is a function on your PowerPoint called "Presenter Tools" under the Slide Show tab. This allows you to see the current slide being projected, the next three slides, and your notes when your laptop is open—while the audience sees only the screen view. Additionally, it has a large digital clock in the upper-left-hand corner that you can also program as a timer.

Some people prefer not to project slides and will opt to hand out paper-based copies of slides. The following are some pros and cons to consider for this approach:

Using Paper-Based PowerPoint Slides

Pros	Cons
No technology worries	You have less control—people can move ahead
People can takes notes as you are talking	Heads are down, meaning less eye contact and personal connection
Tends to be less formal, so it can invite more dialogue	You will present sitting, which is a less powerful position
	Some companies are concerned with unnecessary use of paper
	You cannot manipulate last-minute changes
	You are very limited in your ability to create a unique experience—the audience has "been there, done that"

It is important that you tell your audience when you're presenting with paper-based slides how *they* should use them. For example, you may say, "I know it might be tempting to flip ahead, but if you can stay with me, I will appreciate it." It's also a good idea to occasionally let the audience know, "I am on page 10." This is particularly helpful when you have a rogue audience member bent on going ahead—and in need of an intervention.

iPads

There is a lot of excitement about iPads these days—and why shouldn't there be? They are very cool new products that make our lives a little easier, a lot more entertaining, and definitely more fun. Many of my clients have begun to use them in their sales presentations, while others are still struggling with compliance issues to get approval to use them in theirs.

But before we get too excited about this new toy, let's take a step back and think about how iPads could be best used during a sales presentation. Some people like to use them to send tech-savvy messages to the client—and yes, I agree that they absolutely do this. While I do think there is a role for them in the sales presentation, I do not recommend that they be used for your slides, as so many companies are beginning to do, and here's why: Although there is an app that will allow you (as a presenter) to control the slides that each person sees, you still lose control. This is because you're creating a situation in which every individual is having a relationship with this cool new piece of technology—instead of engaging with *you*. Additionally, the audience can't take notes while viewing your screen as they can when using printed versions of slides. (I am sure that there will be some app that will soon allow you to do so—so this may be a temporary objection.) For these reasons, I suggest that you reserve the use of iPads for short demos or media clips—perhaps a technology demonstration, a video message, or a commercial.

Multimedia

I love to use multimedia in sales presentations—by this, I mean using a mix of PowerPoint, video, audio, and handouts to tell your story. It enriches the audience's experience and can provide an element of the unexpected. In addition, it can help to tell stories that might otherwise be hard to tell. For example, I recently worked with a client company that had typically brought in a technology expert to do a demonstration of its web-based client tools. A common objective of this part of the presentation was to show the client how easy the technology was to use. The obvious question: "If this technology is so easy to use, why do you need a technology expert?" The issue was actually with the demonstration itself. It was a bear to manage, and the technology people that the company brought in to demo the product were not comfortable conducting the overall sales presentation.

We remedied this by incorporating a short video that briefly outlined what tools were available, while showing as well how simple they were to use. Since the company was fighting a reputation in the marketplace of being old and stodgy, we decided to use an edgy animation treatment to counteract the perception. The video, which cost about $10,000 to make, was not only more effective than the live demo, it also paid for itself in no time with the money saved by not having to fly technology experts all over the country. And since the company played it about midway through the presentation, it also contributed to the overall experience by creating an element of surprise for the audience—ultimately working to keep their interest.

I also think it can be effective to use audio for testimonials rather than just projecting quotes in text on a screen. We have done this very effectively for a few of our clients and have been told that it has worked very well in meetings. We have also used audio to tape real calls into a call center, thus giving a feel for the conversation and type of approach that is used.

It is easy and relatively affordable to use multimedia today; the hardest part might be the plethora of options available. When you're trying to decide what medium to use, remember the adage,

"The medium is the message." Make sure that the medium you choose is consistent with the message you want to communicate.

For instance, while I certainly advocate elegance and sophistication, I think that there is a place for high-tech, low-cost contributions. Sometimes a YouTube-type message feels more real and genuine than a highly choreographed, slick video that cost tens of thousands of dollars. At the same time, it can send the message that you get things done quickly and efficiently—and that you are current with today's trends.

Whiteboards and Flip Charts

It does not get lower-tech than the old whiteboards and flip charts. When I was at Chase back in the 1980s, we were quite obsessed with uncovering and studying other investment banks' secrets—particularly those of Goldman Sachs. I remember learning that Goldman actually conducted workshops on how to use flip charts. The idea was to encourage the investment bankers to facilitate strategic dialogues with their clients. They would be skilled at hearing an idea, capturing it on a flip chart, and then mapping out a solution with a client—in the moment.

Although flip charts and whiteboards are low-tech tools, I hope they never go away. While I believe their use is particularly relevant in the earlier stages of the sales cycle, I also think that they can occasionally be used in the sales presentation. For example, as I suggested in Chapter 5, they are great to capture any objectives that clients have put forward during the introductions. They are also helpful for capturing to-do lists or citing outstanding questions that you need to answer, as they signal clients that you are on top of addressing their needs. You can also use them to sketch out a visual for a concept at the moment you're discussing it, which will help people understand it more completely. And an easy way to make these old-school tools into a higher-tech component is to whip out your smartphone or iPad and take a picture of them rather than trying to fold them up with the inevitable tape sticking where you don't want it to—and then jamming it in your briefcase!

> ## CHALLENGE
>
> Review the content categories of your typical presentation. Is there a section that could be better told using audio or video? Is there an appropriate application for an iPad?

Leave-Behinds

Tradition: The slides are the leave-behind.
New tradition: Provide a separate leave-behind.

One of the most frequently asked questions we hear in our presentation workshops is, "How do you use handouts, and when do you hand them out?" Unfortunately, there's no easy answer to this question—and I have learned that some people have strong views on the subject. Before providing a recommendation, let me set some context. First, let's define a few terms:

Handouts: What you provide to the audience to *engage* them in your discussion.

Leave-behinds: Reference information that you provide so that clients can access expanded information, see sample materials, or re-create the presentation, either for themselves or for colleagues after the presentation. These materials *are designed to be read.*

A copy of the slides: Nothing complicated here—these are just that, a copy of the slides so that people can thumb through them as the presenter presents them. At one time, it may have made sense to hand out a copy of the slides for the traditional PowerPoint format (that so many people love to hate). The design of bullet point after bullet point of text made it difficult for people to read what was projected, leaving an abundance of detail to which they could later refer. However, when we approach this from the perspective of creating an engaging experience for our audience, we realize that it no longer makes sense to provide them a copy of the slides. First, there are too many slides with too little information on each; second, the slides don't stand alone; and third, we want the audience to engage with *us*, not with the slides. Remember, slides should be designed to support the presenter, they should not be designed to be read.

Now that we've covered these, let's review a few things we know about materials and how people use them.

1. People cannot read and listen at the same time.
2. Slides are meant to support the presenter. Therefore, slides will not be helpful to anyone in the absence of the presenter.
3. People retain more information when they take notes.
4. Clients often need to reference our presentation and potentially even re-create it for a colleague.

Guidelines for Handouts

- If you choose to use handouts, give the audience only what is necessary for the discussion. Consider distributing them at the very point at which they need them—not before, which might only distract them.
- If the handout is something that clients will take with them, make sure that it can be easily combined with other leave-behinds (e.g., if your leave-behind is in the form of a binder, make sure the handouts are three-hole-punched).

Guidelines for Leave-Behinds

- While we hope that the sales presentation experience lives well beyond the time you spend with the client, the leave-behind serves as a physical reminder. When you are back home, safely tucked into bed, it is possible that one of the decision makers with whom you left your material (or potentially even someone else) is reviewing your leave-behind at that very moment. You therefore want to be certain that this material is sending the messages that you want it to send—from both content and design perspectives.

- Some people choose to provide a flash drive with the information held electronically. The beauty of this approach is that these devices are easy to use, transport, and manipulate at the last minute. The downside is that because they are so small, they aren't always a significant visual reminder of your visit. In the case where you are presenting to clients that have a strong culture of environmental consciousness, electronic materials are almost mandatory. I suggest that you ask clients if they have preference for how they would like to receive additional information, thus eliminating any faux pas in this regard.

Guidelines for Copies of Slides

Following are two options that can work.

A Case for No Slides Most businesspeople have their preferred ways of taking notes; it may be on a legal pad, a spiral notebook, or an iPad. They typically come armed with their device of choice in hand. One thing you can be certain of is that you want their notes to be either connected to your stuff or to theirs. You do not want any notes that they may have taken on some obscure notebook to remain in limbo. For this reason, I am not a proponent of giving people a blank notebook of your choosing for their note taking. Given that the sales presentation's objective is to create an *experience* in which we connect with the client, I prefer *not* to give them slides. In this case, I suggest that the facilitator say something like this at the onset of the presentation: "By design, we have *not* provided you with a handout of the slides, because we would like you to engage with us as we take you through the experience of what it will be like to work with us. Everything that we will review is in a package that we have prepared for you." The client will certainly be able to take down a note or a question in their preferred way.

You may be thinking that this approach is a bit risky. After all, what if they are expecting slides? What if competitors give them slides and handouts and you do not? However, the attractiveness of this approach is that it is *different*. And you know that when you dare to be different, people will remember you!

Abbreviated Slides with Note-Taking Functionality   I have used this approach with some clients effectively. It requires a little prep work, but can be managed efficiently once there is a process in place. The idea is to organize a handout that will allow clients to follow along with the slides and give them the option to take notes—but not necessarily to give them *every* slide. The slides are arranged three to a page; they're categorized by the main topic, with note-taking capability below. Since there is not a lot of detail on each slide, you do not have to worry about the client not being able to read them. This is an effective approach if you think that the client will want to take detailed notes.

The Mundane and the Extraordinary

In addition to the materials that help us to present our story, such as handouts and slides, other materials impact the sales presentation. Some are quite mundane but expected (e.g., business cards), and others can make the sales presentation quite extraordinary (e.g., gifts and custom mementos).

Tent Cards

When you're holding the meeting in your offices, you may choose to use tent cards with each person's name (as placeholders). This is helpful because it allows you to determine in advance exactly where you want everyone to sit. It also helps both the buying committee and the sales team to remember each other's names. Tent cards can be awkward, however, if the presentation is at the client's office. Clients might view it as presumptuous that you're telling them where to sit and providing an unnecessary crutch for remembering names. It can also be very awkward in the setup if they are *already* seated. For these reasons, I typically advise a sales team *not to* use tent cards when they are guests in the clients' offices.

Business Cards

When there are four or more people on the sales team presenting to four or more people on the client team, consider incorporating the business cards in the leave-behind in either a business card sleeve or holder. This will avoid the "Go Fish" scenario of business cards sliding across expansive boardroom tables.

Rolling Out the Red Carpet

I don't care how famous or rich you are, *everyone* likes to feel special. In fact, I have heard that the stars glom on to the goody baskets at the Academy Awards like they have never seen a chocolate-covered Oscar before. Buying committees are no different. An important part of the experience you are creating is making the clients feel special— communicating to them that you want their business and that you are going to pull out all the stops to get it. A great way to do this is to provide a gift or out-of-the-ordinary experience.

What you do obviously depends on your budget, the investment that is warranted, and your ability to access your creative juices. I have seen incredibly elaborate concepts executed; I have also seen low-cost, high-impact ideas that have provided a special and memorable touch. Gifts can give you the opportunity to showcase your creativity and personality. This can be especially poignant when your gift somehow links the client's company to your offering. For example, a sales team presenting to a large hotel chain placed a beautiful silver-plated tray at each person's place. Not only was the hotel known for its service, it was looking for a partner that could provide the same level of service.

In addition to gifts, I have seen very creative ways to set the table for a finals presentation. For a presentation to large American car manufacturer, a woman named Barbara Lewis, head of sales for Prudential Real Estate and Relocation, designed place mats that were meant to mimic Monroney stickers (so named after Mike Monroney, the senator whose bill mandated that dealers display fuel economy, pricing, and other information on the windows of new cars). To highlight their own transparency in pricing, the sales team designed a laminated place mat mimicking a Monroney sticker that outlined all of the deal's characteristics.

The hotel industry sells experience, so it is not surprising that its representatives are thinking about it all the time. Starwood, in particular, very consciously orchestrates all details—from the scent that greets its guests on check-in to the Heavenly Beds that lull them to sleep at night. Ray Hammer, general manager at the Dallas Sheraton (Starwood's largest property), is very aware of the importance of creating extraordinary experiences for companies considering his property for a conference or a meeting. At a recent site visit for Ernst & Young, Starwood demonstrated how it could make the large hotel feel like home for its accounting firm guests by making every touch point feel personalized—from branded hotel keys to customized gift baskets that were constructed to reflect individual preferences. These preferences had been predetermined via a quick multiple-choice quiz that asked questions like this: "If you had thirty minutes of free time, would you rather (a) exercise; (b) take a bath; or (c) read a book." An individual's answer would then dictate if that attendee's basket contained a jump rope, bath salts, or a book. Another question would prompt the guests to choose savory, sweet, or salty, which of course triggered an appropriate snack.

I encourage teams to go beyond the branded pen and push themselves to think creatively about ways to highlight what is special about their offering. However, it is important when you do something like this to strategically position your special gift so that the message is not lost on the client. For example, the person presenting to the hotel chain might say, "We have placed the silver trays before you today to represent your unwavering commitment to provide the highest levels of service to your guests—and our unwavering commitment to provide the same level of service to you." Or the Prudential salesperson might explain, "We have placed a custom-designed Monroney sticker before each of you because we know that you are required to be transparent in your business—something that is important to us as well."

CHALLENGE

Think about a message that you often want to convey to clients (e.g., service, accuracy, value). What small gift or memento could reinforce this?

I encourage teams to get creative and have fun with this. As you do so, consider the following guidelines:

- For the next deal that warrants it, gather a couple of your colleagues and brainstorm a unique gift or experience specific to that client.
- Make sure that whatever you do is of high quality. While the tray used for the hotel chain was not sterling, it looked like it!
- Push yourselves to think of something that will support one of your key messages.
- Practice how you will position your offering so that the meaning is not lost on the buying committee.

If You Remember Only Three Things:

1. Strategically plan the materials for the sales presentation and how you will use them.
2. Consider the use of audio and video to create interest.
3. Make the sales presentation experience extraordinary by providing poignant and memorable gifts.

IV

Twenty-three Elements of the Experience

In this final section before the tool kit, I have outlined all the things—big and small—that have an impact on the sales presentation experience. Some are reminders of many of the ideas throughout the book; others are brand-new thoughts and tips.

1. All Communications Leading Up to the Presentation . . . and the Tone in Which They Are Sent

Every interaction that you have with the client prior to the presentation—every e-mail, telephone call, conference call, and face-to-face meeting—sends a clue about who you are and what you will be like to work with.

Have you ever noticed what cues you pick up in an e-mail from someone you have never met before (or maybe just don't know very well)? There seem to be several different types of e-mailers. Some people prefer to send e-mails that are short and curt; they just get to the point without any salutation or signature. They leave behind basic grammar and literary rules, such as capitalization and punctuation.

On the other extreme are those who are thorough and friendly. They start with some sort of salutation ("Hi John"), then go into a little drum roll ("I hope you are enjoying this beautiful day") before getting to business, and they usually end pleasantly ("Warm regards," "Cheers," or "Thank you").

If you have been through a styles or personality assessment, such as Social Styles, DiSC, or Myers-Briggs, then you are quite familiar the varying communication styles of different personality types—as well as the importance of adjusting your style to fit the person with whom you are communicating. It is critical, particularly in sales, to be as professional and friendly as possible without being verbose. Once you have a dialogue going with a client, you can adjust your style to the client's while maintaining that level of professionalism.

Always make sure that your e-mail's subject line is understandable and updated (i.e., that you're not using the same one left over from the previous e-mail). This is one of the many little things you can do to signal to a client that you are easy to work with.

Conference calls, in particular, are a great way to establish your professionalism and credibility by ensuring that they are well facilitated, which includes the following:

- Provide a well-articulated agenda.
- Be clear about what you want to accomplish.
- Have clarity about the participants' roles.
- Ensure that everyone has a chance to speak.
- Check in with the clients occasionally to confirm that the call is meeting their needs.
- State your name before speaking.
- Start and end on time.

After having worked with many different organizations, I can always get a sense of the organization and what its representatives are like to work based on an early conference call. Your prospects and clients will get the same cues from you as well.

2. How You and Your Team Members Enter the Building and the Room

This can be tricky, especially if the buying committee is already in the room. Ideally, they have taken a break between presentations to allow you to set up; however, this is not always the case. Trying to greet new people while figuring out how to hook up your computer to the projector is tough enough without having to remember what is next. This is why it is important for you to be extremely well organized. Make certain everyone knows exactly what his or her role is in the setup *prior* to the meeting. Use an index card to jot down the steps that you need to take when entering the room. Keep it in a pocket so that it is easily accessible and you don't have to fish through your briefcase to find it.

Juggling beat-up cardboard boxes with briefcases while shaking hands does *not* typically send the message, "We really have our act together." Give some advance thought to how you will carry everything into the room. Consider leaving the cardboard boxes at the hotel and replacing them with branded, lightweight bags that you can easily pack up to bring home after the presentation.

Find out before the presentation whether a client contact is responsible for the meeting's logistics. If so, develop a relationship with him or her. Find out as much as possible about the logistics:

- Is parking available?
- Check on access to the building, including security requirements.
- What are the room characteristics?
  Size
  Setup (table type, location of screen)
  Special considerations (very large, very small, odd shape)
- Find out attendees' names and roles (including pronunciation/ spelling, if necessary).
- Will anyone be attending remotely? If so, via telephone or teleconference? Will they need materials in advance? Assign someone on the team to look out for this person during the presentation so he or she is not forgotten.
- Check on the scheduling. Is there a presentation or a meeting before yours? If so, will participants be taking a break? When can you have access to the room?

3. How You Greet People When You Enter the Room

It is a good idea to develop a strategy for how you will greet people when you enter the room. While it always makes sense to shake as many hands as possible, this can be a challenge if you're facing a large buying committee whose members are already sitting. Again, the more you know about the room setup and the presentation's scheduling, the better you will be able to strategize your approach with the team and avoid an awkward greeting.

A NOTE ON HANDSHAKES

Professionals know how important their handshake is. And most of us assume we have a good one. While this may seem rudimentary, even insulting (forgive me if this is the case), do not assume. I am amazed how many supposedly seasoned hands I shake that are either lacking in firmness or have too much substance.

I recently found out from my husband and sons that there is a certain manly perception surrounding handshakes, almost like a secret code. I did not initially want to believe this until other men also confirmed it. They told me that it is common for men to pull a power play through their handshake to signal dominance. If this sounds familiar, I suggest that you drop it for the sales presentation.

I have also had men shake my hand as if I am made of china. Believe me, I am not, and some women could be insulted by this (not to mention the fact that it just feels awful). So, gentlemen, although you might consider this a kindness, go ahead and give us women a firm handshake. Trust me—we can handle it.

Double handshakes should be reserved for Bill Clinton and grandmothers. For the rest of us, they reek of trying too hard and are a little too cozy for the boardroom.

4. Where You Choose to Sit

This, of course, is easiest to handle when you're on your own turf. In most cases, however, you won't be. Let's start with the ideal scenario. In a typical boardroom situation, the person who leads the meeting is ideally seated at the front of the room, stage left (if there is a screen). Again, the rationale is that the person presenting should be to the left of the screen, because we read from left to right (i.e., it is natural for them to glance at the screen and back again at the presenter). The person facilitating the meeting (usually the salesperson or the relationship or account manager) should sit where he or she has the best view of everyone in the room. A general rule of thumb is to avoid, as much as possible, having to move our heads from left to right to see the entire audience.

ROOM SETUP

It often makes sense to sit the sales team across from the client team, since this allows everyone to have a clear view of the other team members. People often believe that you should mix it up to avoid the visual of being at opposite sides of the table. While this is a good strategy for a business dinner, it is not the best for a presentation. It is more important in this situation for people to be able to see the presenter, and vice versa.

It is often a good idea to have people sit in the order in which they are presenting.

5. The Room's Physical Setup

You often do not have much control over this, since you will be presenting at the client's site more often than not. You can, however, get as much information about the room as possible before the presentation in order to prepare in advance. If you have access to the room before the client arrives, you can also make minor adjustments to shades, lighting, and seating. Sometimes people think they need to dim lights when using a projector; however, this is rarely the case. Do not sacrifice a bright, cheery room for perfectly crisp projection. I'd rather have the slides a little faded than risk my audience fading as they sit in a room that suggests it is nap time.

6. How You Open the Presentation

The energy and enthusiasm that the first speaker conveys has the potential to impact the *entire* presentation. He or she sets the tone, or climate, for the meeting. This person's warmth, smile, personality, and confidence will all contribute to those important opening minutes that will set the client's first impression of the team and your organization. The level of formality or informality exhibited will influence the tone for the entire meeting.

7. How You Facilitate the Meeting Throughout

The professionalism with which you run the meeting from beginning to end is critical to the sales presentation's success. This includes how you manage time, involve people, handle questions, make transitions, and maintain the integrity of the agenda. Time is often an issue for sales teams, as they do not know for certain how many questions or comments the buying committee will have for each section. When facilitators realize that they are at risk of going overtime, I advise that they ask the client for help in determining how to allocate the rest of the agenda. This will give you some insight into what is most important to the client, help you manage the time, and demonstrate your desire to focus on the client's needs.

8. The Team's Personality and Energy

Again, the warmth and personality of the team is critical here. The more you can show your personalities and set a climate for the clients to show theirs, the better the meeting will be—and the more likely you will be to achieve a positive outcome.

9. The Materials and Equipment You Use . . . and How You Use Them

PowerPoint slides, paper-based handouts, three-ring binders, spiral-bound booklets, videos, demos, presentation cards, flip charts, whiteboards, laptops, and iPads are all potential sales presentation tools. As discussed in detail in Chapter 12, what you choose to use will have an impact on the experience you create. On one of the first deals I coached, the person presenting the technology capability had prepared presentation boards with screen shots for his presentation (really, I am not making this up). I asked him what kind of a message he thought that his choice of delivery would send to the client—which was something I think he later recalled as an "aha" moment. Remember, *the medium is the message*. Ask yourself whether the medium you are using is sending the message you want it to.

10. The Team's Behavior . . . and Consistency between the Behavior and the Message

In item 9, you can see an example of a message ("We are technologically savvy") that conflicts with a team member's behavior (putting slides on presentation boards). Remember, no matter what you say, your behavior trumps words.

For example, if you want to send a message that you are creative, make sure that you are behaving creatively in the sales presentation. If one of your key messages is that you can make the complex simple, you need to be extra conscious of eliminating complex charts and graphs.

11. How You Present Your Business Card

If you have worked with the Japanese, you know how important they consider the presentation of the business card. The presenter holds it with both hands by its corners and facing out, so that the receiver can read it. It is considered impolite if the receiver either does not look at the card as it is presented or casually tosses it in a bag or on the table. Americans, on the other hand, tend to carelessly pass business cards to each other without so much as a quick glance. While we do not have to be as strict as the Japanese in an American sales setting, it makes sense to be conscious of receiving a client's business card with respect.

12. The Quality of Paper on Which Things Are Presented

The next time you go to Nordstrom's, notice the quality of paper used for the receipts. It is a cut above any other receipt out there. I expect that this is because, like so much of what Nordstrom does, it wants the experience to be a cut above the rest. The little things make a difference and get noticed. Many companies provide a giveaway in their presentations—a pen, a notepad, a flash drive. If you do this, take a step back and think about what your offering communicates. A notepad may not be the best choice if you are presenting to an environmentally conscious company.

I recently worked on a deal where sales team gave away a fancy pen packaged in a box that had a small "Made in Japan" label at the end. Since the client was an American car company, this didn't convey the best message—or one that the buying committee would particularly welcome, so we decided to take the pens out of their boxes.

13. The Attire of the People Presenting

We are often asked about wardrobe for a sales presentation. Even if you are presenting to a casually attired company, you should err on the side of formality—typically one step up from their dress code. It is a good idea to ask in advance of the presentation what the dress code is so that you can provide direction to the team members.

In some situations, the sales presentation can bring a variety of people from your organization to the table. Some may interface with clients on a regular basis, and others may not see clients at all—except for during the presentation. There is often less need for these people to invest in a business wardrobe—and it can sometimes be a challenge for them to select the right outfit. The easiest wardrobe direction is to wear a suit and to keep it simple. Call me old-fashioned, but earrings should be limited to women's ears only (as opposed to various other body parts)—and left at home entirely for men.

14. Team Photos

If your presentation or handouts include pictures of team members, make sure that they are current and consistent in look and feel. This is one of those little things that can make a big impression. Believe it or not, one organization I worked with used its security pictures for client materials. They looked like they had been taken at the local penitentiary. What were they thinking?

15. How You Take Notes . . . and What You Take Them with and On

There are actually three components to this: (1) whether and how you take notes, (2) what you are writing with, and (3) what you are writing on. These might sound like insignificant details, but again, we are talking about the culmination of *a lot* of details that come together to create the whole experience. A chewed pencil is probably not consistent with the message you want to send, and neither is a worn yellow legal pad. If you use paper to take notes, use a nice notebook or portfolio to hold your pad. People now take notes on iPads, which offers some great apps that support note taking. The iPad is sleek and sends a message that you embrace and are comfortable with current technology. However, if you are using the keyboard, be careful that it does not swallow you up. I have found that iPads can demand a lot more attention from the user than the old pen-and-paper method— attention that might prevent you from connecting with your audience.

16. How You Advance Slides

As I mentioned in Chapter 12, presenters who don't advance their own slides put themselves at a great disadvantage by ceding control to someone else. It can be distracting and look quite sloppy to the audience—so make sure everyone on the sales force is equipped with a slide advancer!

17. How You Handle the Unexpected

If you have been in sales for any length of time, I am sure you have a few stories about the unexpected occurring. Whether it is mishaps with technology, coffee spilling on a laptop, a teammate freezing, materials not arriving, torrential downpours as you are unloading, or a pen that leaks in your pocket (I'm getting stressed just thinking about all this!), you know by now that sometimes stuff happens. While we obviously want to do our best to plan for every possible scenario, we know we can't plan for everything. The way in which we address these moments of unwelcome surprise becomes part of the client's experience.

The good news is that clients are human, too, and will likely be empathetic toward a situation that is not in your control—*if* you handle it with grace, composure, and a sense of humor. A colleague of mine tells about a fire alarm that went off about 10 minutes into her presentation. It took over an hour to get everyone back in the room, which left her with only about 20 minutes of the allocated time. A competitor was scheduled to come in almost directly after. Rather than rushing through or asking the competitor to wait, she offered to reschedule. The client was enormously grateful for the team's flexibility. My colleague won the business and now that they are working together closely, she and her client often kid about that eventful day.

18. How You Close

Your close is your lasting impression. It is critical to the success of the sales presentation. Because time can be so challenging for a sales team to manage, the close often gets short shrift. But if you do nothing else, *close well!* It is the most important part of the meeting. Give the client reasons to do business with you. The exercise from Chapter 3, "How to Choose Just Three," will help you structure your close so that you are able to articulate it in just 30 seconds if you have to.

19. How and When You Leave the Room

Scrambling in the final minutes of the presentation to gather your things and hurriedly say your good-byes so the next team can present is awkward. This is easier, of course, if the team takes a break and gives you a few minutes to pack up and leave. Knowing what the situation will be in advance of the presentation will help you be prepared, so have a plan, and try to leave gracefully.

20. Your Postpresentation Follow-Up

Just as all communication leading up to the presentation contributes to the overall experience, so does the communication that happens *after* the presentation. It is just as important to develop a follow-up strategy as it is to strategize for the sales presentation itself. It is not unusual to have some tactical follow-ups that have to do with the facts and the figures. It may be a different pricing scenario or an answer to a specific question about the technology platform. Of course, getting these kinds of questions is a good sign; they signal that the client is leaning toward choosing you. This kind of tactical follow-up is critical and must be handled carefully and urgently.

I encourage teams to think about things outside of the tactical follow-ups by asking, "How can we extend the emotional experience beyond the boardroom?" For example, for a presentation to McDonald's, I took a picture of the team in front of the local golden arches, holding up their lunches. We then made the photo into a thank-you card and sent it to all the committee members with a handwritten note. Just before the Bank of New York merged with Mellon, my firm was in a competitive bidding situation for a large piece of business for Bank of New York's private bank. I managed to mix a baseball analogy and a golf analogy during the presentation, which made the entire room roar with laughter at my expense and then continue to rib me throughout the meeting. (I have since learned to stay away from all sports analogies.) After the presentation, I sent custom golf balls that read, "Let us hit it out of the park!"

While we certainly want to limit the errors we make in front of clients, sometimes they can provide an opportunity for follow-up!

21. Your Patience while Waiting for the Decision

One of the hardest things for salespeople to do is to be patient. Because it's their job to *make things happen*, it is practically in their DNA to push a deal to close.

You certainly want to be attentive to your client's needs for additional information after a presentation. And you certainly want to send every signal possible that you want the business (without looking desperate, of course). So, what do you do when clients have all the information they need, and they just don't move? *You wait.* I know, it's hard, and I hate it, too! But it's a critical part of the process.

Several years ago, I had coached a team that was presenting to a large manufacturing company. While the salesman didn't tell me this outright, I was fairly certain that the presentation's result was going to either make or break his year. I knew that this was important— *really* important. So I worked with his team and did everything I could to help with their messaging, materials, and skills.

When we debriefed after the presentation, I learned that the client had provided very positive feedback, to the tune of, "Yours was the best presentation by far!" The salesman had also received some very positive feedback from a third party who told him, "It's in the bag." The client had communicated some buy signals by requesting specific information related to pricing. The team was feeling great. The champagne was practically on ice.

Well it is good that it wasn't—because it would have been sitting in lukewarm water for a long time. About six weeks after the presentation, the salesman called me to ask what he should do about the delay. I spent some time with him reviewing what he had already done. He had sent the follow-up requested by the client, and he had checked in a week later, asking for an update. He was told that everyone was going crazy dealing with a recent reorganization, and they couldn't be pulled away. He called again the following week and learned that the buying committee members still hadn't had a chance to get together. The weeks went on in similar fashion. In the meantime, he did the best that he could to keep in touch by providing a couple of relevant articles.

By the time he called me, his phone calls to the client weren't even being returned. He was feeling desperate, and he needed to do something.

Although I knew it was not what he wanted to hear, I told him that he was at risk of crossing the line from being client-centered to being self-centered. One of the things that the client reps had appreciated and commented on was how attuned both he and the team had been to their needs. Well, what the client needed at this point was to focus on other things—which was in direct conflict with the sales-person's need to close the deal. I knew that if he crossed that line, if he put his need before the client's, it could damage the deal and his reputation.

Unfortunately, the deal did not close. The client's rep called about a month later to tell him that, although he and his team had been the clear winners, the buying committee had decided to sit tight until things settled down. The company rep thanked him for his patience.

Shortly following that exchange, the salesman sent a personal note to each of the buying committee members, which simply stated that he knew how important timing was and that it had to be right. He added that he and the team enjoyed meeting each of them and learning about their company. He included a picture of his sales team with a caption that read, "We're ready when you are."

About six months later, the company was in the news for making a significant acquisition. About six months after that, the salesman was contacted to submit a response to an abbreviated RFP. While things had changed, the client was now ready to move, and they needed pricing to reflect the larger scope of the project. The deal closed in record time, and it was significantly larger than originally anticipated.

It's amazing to think what a little patience can do for you.

22. The Amount of Effort and Creativity You Bring to the Table

Buyers want to know that you want their business. Demonstrating your desire to work with them by going the extra mile can contribute greatly to a win. No matter how sophisticated a client, most people like a gift or a takeaway. If the size of the deal warrants it, you may want to consider a small investment in something that is customized for the client. As outlined in Chapter 12, it is always a good idea to find ways that your gift can reinforce a key message.

Tokens of appreciation do not have to come in the form of gifts. They could be anything that shows you have gone the extra mile to do something special for the client (e.g., a videotaped message from the president of your company before the meeting, a photo thank-you card after the meeting).

23. Site Visits

Depending on your industry, the sales cycle may culminate in a site visit. Sometimes the visit is intended to justify the buying team's decision, and other times it is intended to assist them in making the final decision. Either way, this is a situation where the selling team clearly needs to shine.

There are some significant advantages to a site visit: It takes place on your turf, so you have much greater control than you do in a sales presentation. As hosts, you get to determine the day's agenda and the layout. You also have more flexibility with the scheduling.

The site visit is an opportunity to create the ultimate experience in which you can demonstrate to the client what it would be like to work with your organization. Where the sales presentation is akin to a snapshot, the site visit is more like a movie. It is a situation in which the client reps are observing and experiencing many more details: the reception that greets them at the door, how security is handled, the elevator ride to the offices, the tours they are given, the way introductions are facilitated on the tours, and the spaces they are in. If breakfast or lunch is served, the menu, seating arrangements, and attendees from your firm are all important components. You must ensure that every single detail communicates to the buying committee how wonderful you will be to work with—and how much you will value them as a client.

The Tool Kit

The following tools have been designed to make it as simple as possible for you to apply the concepts in this book. You can download and customize them for your use at www.precisionsalescoaching.com and www.makeitallaboutthem.com.

Tools

The Sales Presentation Checklist

Designed as a quick reference for the salesperson, it captures all of the critical activities that are involved before and after a sales presentation.

The Intelligence List

A list of information to gather in advance of the sales presentation.

The Timeline

A framework that you can use to plan the activities and timeline associated with a sales presentation.

The Storyboard

To be used by the salesperson to map out the entire presentation, and by individual team members to map out their section of the presentation.

The Strategy Session

Suggested agenda, objective, and approach for facilitating the strategy session, which is designed to capture the messages, timing, and agenda for the sales presentation.

The Rehearsal

Suggested agenda, objectives and approach for facilitating the rehearsal.

The Big Day

To be used on the day of the sales presentation to remember all the little details.

The Debrief

To be used after the sales presentation to capture client information and insights from the team, solidify next steps, and assess the team's performance.

THE SALES PRESENTATION CHECKLIST

Congratulations! You have been invited to present. Use this checklist to be certain you remember every detail.

UPON NOTICE, OR BEFORE IN ANTICIPATION OF AN INVITATION TO PRESENT

☐ Elicit insight and logistical information from the client

☐ Determine who will be invited from your company

☐ Inform team and others who will be supporting the deal

☐ Develop timeline, send to team

☐ Prepare for strategy call

☐ Determine and share logistics with team (strategy session, rehearsals)

☐ Determine three key messages

☐ Create storyboard; send grid to each presenter

☐ Determine slides and handouts

☐ Send any important updates to the team

☐ Consider any unusual circumstances: logistics, decision makers who will not be present

PREPARATION FOR THE STRATEGY SESSION

☐ Develop first draft of presentation (including agenda slide, needs slide, closing slide); determine time allocation for each section

☐ Send any important updates to the team

☐ Conduct strategy session— either in a group (preferred) or with people individually

PREPARATION FOR THE REHEARSAL

☐ Obtain any necessary approvals (legal, compliance)

☐ Finalize slides and materials

☐ Confirm time, location, logistics, and equipment with client contact

☐ Conduct rehearsal

AFTER THE PRESENTATION

☐ Facilitate the debrief

☐ Manage follow-up with the client

☐ Keep the team informed

THE INTELLIGENCE

I assume that by this point you have already conducted a thorough needs analysis. Therefore, this checklist is specific to the preparation for the presentation. Use it as a prompt on important information to gather by answering the following questions:

☐ Why were you selected as a finalist? What did the clients like about you? Did they express any concerns?

☐ Who are your competitors? How many have been invited to present?

☐ What will it take for you to win?

☐ Do you know the decision-making process? Will they be using a scorecard? Are there any decision makers who will not be present?

☐ What is the order of presentations? (Request to go last; if you cannot go last, then request to go first.)

☐ Who will be on the buying committee? What are their roles? What have you learned from LinkedIn and other research? How would you describe the personality of the group? What moles and/or coaches can you engage to gain insight?

☐ How much time will you have to present? Will the buying committee be issuing an agenda?

☐ Do you know the room in which the presentations will be conducted? What is its shape, and what are the typical seating arrangements?

THE TIMELINE

Customize this timeline to your specific client situation.

Date	Action item	Responsible	Comments

THE STORYBOARD

This storyboard is used for two purposes:

1. For the salesperson to create an overall agenda for reference by the team

2. For each presenter to organize his or her part of the presentation

Big Three Messages

1.

2.

3.

Topic	Critical Points	Opportunities to Reinforce the Big Three	Proof Points, Differentiators, Stories, and Metaphors

THE STRATEGY SESSION

The Strategy Session is the opportunity for the team to review messaging, timing, and materials before the big day. You should conduct this at least a week before the sales presentation and provide all the information required for the team to hit the rehearsal ready to rehearse in character.

Objectives:

- To determine the presentation flow, the key messages for each section and how the team will reinforce the Big Three messages
- To review any logistics
- To update the team on any new client information

Materials Required:

- ☐ Main storyboard (prepared by salesperson)
- ☐ Slides and handouts
- ☐ Individual storyboards (prepared by each presenter)

Strategy Session Agenda:

Welcome, review agenda

Review Big Three messages

Review what you know about buying committee (roles, personality, interests)

Review agenda for presentation and associated timing (storyboard)

Each individual provides an overview of his or her presentation, with an emphasis on the key messages and differentiators

After each person discusses his or her section, the salesperson and other team members share their suggestions

Brainstorm difficult questions, determine appropriate responses, and assign responsibility

Plan introductions (with an emphasis on credibility and personality) and transitions (passing off to a colleague so that the client is excited to hear from him/her)

Confirm expectations and logistics for rehearsal and sales presentation

THE REHEARSAL

The rehearsal is the opportunity for the team to refine their presentation and build confidence for their flawless delivery. A minimum of one full day is typically required.

Objective:

To ensure that the team is fully prepared for all aspects of the presentation

Materials:

☐ Presentation
☐ Handouts
☐ Flip charts
☐ Projector
☐ Slide Advancer
☐ Any other materials that will be used in the finals

Agenda:

Welcome and warm-up (the benefit of the warm-up is that it helps set the climate and chemistry of the team)

Review ground rules and post them

Review client updates and new information

Review agenda, outline, and timing of presentation; assign timekeeper role

Review seating and logistics

Conduct each section of the presentation, time it, and provide feedback

Practice question and answers in character (either with each section or at the end of the rehearsal)

Conduct a full rehearsal without interruption. Provide feedback at the end of the presentation

Sample Ground Rules:

- Keep the objective in mind at all times: *to win the deal.*
- Provide balanced feedback—what is working and ideas for improvement.
- Provide specific feedback on what works and ideas for improvement.

THE BIG DAY

Review this checklist with the team to help you to remember all the little things.

BEFORE THE MEETING

- ☐ Double-check location, time and security procedures for building access
- ☐ Check equipment—ensure a team member has a backup computer and copy of presentation
- ☐ Get pumped!

UPON ENTERING THE ROOM

- ☐ Seat the team according to plan
- ☐ Distribute materials
- ☐ Hook up and test computer, projector, slide advancer

DURING THE MEETING (THE LITTLE THINGS)

- ☐ Confirm the amount of time allocated for the presentation with the client
- ☐ Refrain from titles in introductions; show personality
- ☐ Facilitate introductions—the sales team first, then buying committee members (name, area of responsibility, what each wants to get out of meeting)
- ☐ Try to acknowledge appropriate committee members when referring to their area of interest
- ☐ Build credibility of team members when passing the floor to them
- ☐ When calling a colleague to speak (unplanned) give him or her a heads-up ("In a minute I will ask John to comment, but before I do . . .")

DURING THE MEETING (THE LITTLE THINGS)

☐ When answering a question, check back with the person who posed it to make sure you addressed it

☐ Enthusiastically support the team; smile, nod, laugh when appropriate

☐ Be passionate and have fun!

THE DEBRIEF

Debrief within 48 hours of the finals.

Objectives:

- To capture information and insight that is important to close the deal
- To capture what went well and practices that you want to repeat for the next sales presentation
- To identify areas for improvement

Agenda:

- Review any updates and feedback with the team.
- Capture client information.
  - ☐ What did we learn?

  - ☐ What else can we do to move the deal forward?

  - ☐ How can we elicit more feedback?

  - ☐ What are the next steps

  - ☐ Who is taking care of thank-you tasks and follow-up?

- Critique team performance.
  - ☐ What should we keep doing?

  - ☐ What should we stop doing?

  - ☐ What should we start doing to make our next performance better?

Index